D1564726

The Acadians:
Creation of a People

Pg 31 ✳ ✳

THE FRONTENAC LIBRARY
GENERAL EDITOR—GEOFFREY MILBURN
Althouse College of Education
University of Western Ontario

The Acadians:
Creation of a People

Naomi Griffiths

McGRAW-HILL RYERSON LIMITED

Toronto   Montreal   New York   London   Sydney
Johannesburg   Mexico   Panama   Düsseldorf
Singapore   Rio de Janeiro   Kuala Lumpur   New Delhi

THE ACADIANS: CREATION OF A PEOPLE

Library of Congress Catalog Card Number 72-9529

ISBN 0-07-092966-1

3 4 5 6 7 8 9 10 AP-72 10 9 8 7 6 5

Printed and bound in Canada

Contents

Maps and Illustrations

Acknowledgements

The publisher wishes to acknowledge with gratitude those who have given their permission to use copyrighted material in this book. Every effort has been made to credit all sources correctly. The author and publisher will welcome information that will allow them to correct any errors or omissions.

Where necessary, permission to quote copyrighted materials has been sought through the publishers noted in the appropriate places.

The illustrations in this book have been obtained from the following sources: The Trustees of the British Museum, pp. 26, 38; the Public Archives of Canada p. 29; photographs by W. R. Dionne, pp. 5, 68, 81, 83 — copyright W. R. Dionne; N. E. S. Griffiths, sketch map, p. 1; State Archives, Harrisburg, Pennsylvania, p. 66 — with thanks to the Archivist.

Cover: From photo taken in the summer of 1969, somewhere south of Digby, Nova Scotia.

Many people become involved in the writing of a book. My colleagues at Carleton University encouraged me; Mrs. Diane Millar helped with the final checking of the footnotes, and the preparation of the Index: Joseph Kukulka aided with the photographs; the Canada Council grant enabled me to gather material for the concluding pages, which led me to a new understanding of the Acadians in exile; and Mr. N. J. Press, of Barclays Bank, further eased the troubles of study in small French villages by an enlightened financial policy. McGraw-Hill Ryerson have been most patient with circumstances that delayed the completion of this manuscript and my thanks are, above all, due especially to Geoffrey Milburn, who is that rare being, a helpful critic.

N. E. S. GRIFFITHS

To D. M. L. Farr and
Mme. Albert Dionne (née Edna Leblanc) :
two friends who have given me continuous
encouragement

Foreword

The story of the Acadians in the eighteenth century is both dramatic and haunting. One of the earliest settlements in North America, Acadia grew from humble beginnings to a community of some eight thousand souls whose habits and culture remained distinct from their French-speaking but distant neighbours in Quebec. Forty years after the British assumed control of the region came tragedy. Ever since 1755 people in all walks of life have asked themselves why it was necessary to remove the greater proportion—about 6,000—of these French-speaking inhabitants of what is now Nova Scotia and New Brunswick from their homes to be scattered in many locations in the New World and the Old. The very concept of deportation — with, in this case, its accompanying human misery — is so repugnant that many attempts have been made to assign responsibility and guilt. And, when set in the larger context of Canadian history, it could not be forgotten that the people deported were French-speaking Catholics; those deporting English-speaking Protestants.

The Acadians were the first large group of French-speaking people in the New World to be ruled by Britain. After moving more than once from French to British control in the seventeenth century, they were finally absorbed into the Old British Empire at the Treaty of Utrecht. Their tragedy was presaged in their location and the intricate manoevres of eighteenth-century global politics. Caught in the crossroads — and crossfire — of imperial rivalries, the Acadians lands became strategically vital to the ambitions of England, France and the inhabitants of the American colonies. Since the status of the Acadians was a matter of dispute, their security was threatened as war fever grew. In the administration of Governor Lawrence, the last threads of trust between ruler and ruled snapped.

This epic story has come to us in many forms, some written by scholars of repute, others by poets or politicians, and not a few by propagandists. Longfellow's *Evangeline,* published almost a century after deportation, became enormously popular and its engaging myths gave form to Acadian national feeling. English and French historians have provided alternative explanations that did not necessarily come closer to what actually happened. The telling of the story is often as influential as the actions of contemporary participants.

In *The Acadians: Creation of a People,* Naomi Griffiths has attempted not only to recover for us the character of the Acadian experience but also to assess the contributions of those writers who precede her. Since her account is rooted in a profound knowledge of contemporary evidence, she has been able to cast the story in a new light. It is a personal and moving introduction to what the author calls on the one hand "a story of human passion and obstinacy" and on the other "a gloriously awkward compendium of exceptions to everybody's rules". Read for its own sake, the story of Acadia reveals yet another dimension to the human experience. Set in a Canadian context, it is a troubling reminder of what happens when two cultures meet. On the latter subject we have listened to the same tune on many an occasion — and failed to learn much about the score.

G. MILBURN

Introduction

Acadian history provides Canada with one of her most rich and magnificently complicated heritages. It is a story of human passion and obstinacy, an affirmation of individual courage and beliefs, a statement of the rights of small settlements against the claims of large Empires, and, above all, a gloriously awkward compendium of exceptions to everybody's rules. The original Acadian settlers did not come, as might be thought, just from one area of France, nor even from France alone. Among the original settlers to be called Acadian were bad-tempered Scottish farmers with a tendency to tell government officials to mind their own business and Irish sailors with an eye for pretty women. There were Basque fishermen with a capacity for absorbing vast quantities of alcohol and dyke-builders from the Atlantic coast of France as well as a distant cousin of the great Cardinal Richelieu, bent on founding a fortune. The original settlers were not only a mixture of people from different states, they were also a mixture of Catholics and Protestants. Further, the colony that was founded, to which the Acadians belonged, was never the exclusive concern of only one European power during the seventeenth century. As early as 1621 it had two names, "Acadie or Nova Scotia" and under this joint title both France and England claimed it.

It is not surprising that with such a wide variety of influences in their lives the Acadians built a distinct community for themselves during the seventeenth century, one that was separate from other colonies in North America and one that had a large measure of independence from Europe. The early impact of New England on the Acadians and the growth of English influence on them during the seventeenth century, an influence which was much strengthened during the fourteen years, 1656-1670, when the colony was part of the British Empire, were factors which helped to make the Acadians substantially different from the French settlers along the St. Lawrence. Yet this part of Acadian history has remained relatively unknown. The drama of their deportation in 1755, when the majority of Acadians were exiled from Nova Scotia has over-shadowed the slower and more complex saga of their earlier history. But the deportation neither created nor destroyed the Acadians. It has been the most obviously striking event in Acadian history, but it could not have occurred had there been no Acadians. That is to say, the events of 1755 happened because the French-speaking population of Nova Scotia of that time was not merely another French settlement, temporarily controlled by the English. In 1755 the Acadians already had their own identity.

This identity survived the searing consequences of the failure of Acadian political action in 1755. Although the deportation took place, leaving the Acadian population of Nova Scotia less than a thousand in 1760, there were over eight thousand Acadians in New Brunswick and Nova Scotia by 1800. Further, the Acadian community retained its distinctiveness throughout the nineteenth century. Even after the French Canadian convention which took place in 1880, the Acadian élite argued for the separate development of their people. At the Acadian convention which took place in Memramcook in 1881, and which selected an Acadian national holiday, more than one speaker clearly outlined the choice for the Acadians. As S. J. Doucet said:[1]

> Do we (Acadians) wish to become linked with the Canadians in such a way as to be no longer recognised as a separate people? . . . then let us choose Saint Jean-Baptiste, the national holiday of the Canadians as our own. . . . Should we, on the other hand, wish to preserve our national group and at the same time profit from an efficacious and unique means of strengthening and affirming our existance as a separate people? Then let us choose our own national holiday taking account only of ourselves . . . . After we will be united on another plane, the plane of a higher politic, much above those of particularism — the plane where we all French Canadian, English, Scots, Irish are united together by the bonds of the great Canadian confederation.

As the nineteenth century drew to a close the Acadians could signify their sense of united identity to others through a flag, the tricolour with the papal star, a holiday, the Assumption, and a hymn, "Ave Maria Stella". The force of Acadian development had survived all hazards. Yet at no time was there a politically independent and sovereign state of Acadie.

The fascination of Acadian history, then, is more than just in the interest of human survival against great odds. It is in the fascination of the phenomenon of national feelings. What created Acadie? What was Acadie at any given time? What does it mean to be an Acadian? This book is an attempt to ask such questions in the context of the adventure of the actual happenings of Acadian history.

N. E. S. GRIFFITHS.
Ottawa, May 1972.

Chapter I

The Making of a People: 1604-1710

The story of the Acadians has its beginnings in the seventeenth century, with the building of little villages along the shores of the Bay of Fundy. It is the story of how European settlement came to those lands which today form part of the Canadian Maritime provinces and the northeastern part of the American state of Maine. It is about the way in which the lives led by the

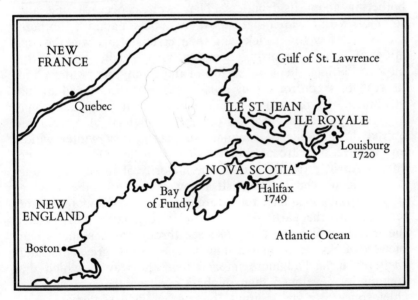

settlers and their descendants created a new and unique community, with its own particular traditions, its own patterns of political action and its own forms of social obligations. In 1600, no one called themselves, or anyone else, an Acadian. In 1700, however, a great many people used the word "Acadian" in talking of the inhabitants of that "continental cornice"[1] between the territories claimed by New France and New England, in debating whether the most important characteristics of this new community were its links with France, or its trading activities with New England, or its military possibilities, or its religious beliefs. There was no question about the actual existence of the Acadians in 1700; what was in question, and so remains, was exactly who they were.

The major determinants of the character of the Acadian community were the lands which the Acadians actually settled, the European backgrounds from which the first settlers came, and the interest in the affairs of the Acadians displayed by France and England. The exact limits of the territory open to exploitation as "Acadie" was always a matter of debate. But for those who settled Acadie the question had no urgency; they had enough problems to solve in the centre of the land without bothering about its frontiers. They were concerned first and foremost with the area that is now Nova Scotia and the southern section of New Brunswick, and their common aim was the creation of a self-supporting community. The land became the most stable ingredient in the life of the colony, its produce and its resources controlling in great measure future Acadian development. Its climate made demands, for it precluded some activities just as it enforced others: it blighted vines and required the building of adequate shelters against winter winds and the frequent frosts, which came from late October to the end of April. From the outset, the majority of those who came to Acadie wanted to establish a new homeland rather than a trading station or a base for future exploration of a more distant territory. So the particular hills and rivers, lakes and forests, the way in which the earth met sea through a coastline which blended rocky shore and sandy beaches, stark grey cliffs and sheltered bays, had more impact upon the way in which the community developed than might have been the case had the chief concern of the migrants been other than settlement.

But the Acadians developed as more than merely transplanted Europeans, as more than people who fundamentally retained a way of life which their ancestors had moulded in another time and another place. Those who settled these lands came from all over France, from Scotland, from Ireland, from

England and even from Portugal. The way in which diverse traditions and languages were welded together is as important a part of the making of the Acadians as is the land they developed, and which became so beloved. Acadian customs and techniques were built up with the knowledge brought by migrants from widely differing backgrounds, who adapted their skills to the demands of a new land. Men who had learnt how to drain fresh-water swamps now worked on seawater flats, moving from the fields of the Loire to the shores of the Bay of Fundy. Wine-growers from La Rochelle, masons from Poitier and sailors from the Basque country now turned their talents to building birch canoes, to tracking the forests and to farming unfamiliar soil. It is probable that such a mixture in such a setting would of its own have produced a community unlike any other. However, there was a third and equally powerful force acting upon events. Land and migrants did not build Acadie in isolation. France and England, as well as New France and New England, regarded the colony with interest and their politicians, their administrators and their business men attempted to manipulate Acadian affairs to suit their own interests. The migration of the sixteenth and seventeenth centuries from Europe to America was no simple movement of separate individuals or separate groups of individuals. Such voyages took place, but the migration essentially entailed the expansion of the European scene, politically, religiously, economically and culturally. Those who settled on the new lands found that not only the way in which they built their societies, but the very societies themselves, were deeply influenced by the continuing pressure upon them of the lands they had left behind. And each new society established in the Americas tended to alter the situation of those already there.

It was the French who first sent an expedition to settle that part of America which would produce the Acadians. They used the Indian name of the lands, and spelt it on their maps in many different ways, such as "la cadie", and "LaCadye".[2] In 1603, Henry IV, then King of France, granted patents to a Protestant nobleman, Pierre du Gast, Sieur de Monts, which named him viceroy and captain-general "on sea and land in La Cadie, Canada and other parts of New France between 40° and 60°.[3] De Monts was granted the right to control the fur-trade as a means of financing his venture, and he fitted out two ships to set out in the spring of 1604 to exploit his opportunity. In the late summer of that year he left seventy-nine men to winter on Ste. Croix Island in Passamaquoddy Bay, on the north shore of the Bay of Fundy, promising to return in the spring of the following year with new supplies for them. Among those left was Samuel de Champlain and from his diary one learns of the terrible winter the men endured.

More than half the company died of scurvy and the rest were very greatly weakened by the disease. The site of their camp had a poor water supply and not enough timber for fuel. The cold was so intense that the cider was divided by an axe and measured out by the pound. Only the cheap red Spanish wine remained unfrozen. When spring finally came, in early April, and late for that part of the world, it was obvious that a new site must be found if a permanent settlement was to be established. A search for a better location, however, could not begin immediately. Unless de Monts returned, as promised, with new supplies, it would be wiser for Champlain and his companions to try and return to France. Their chances of surviving the next winter without relief from Europe were thin. They did not know enough about their environment to be self-sufficient at this stage.

De Monts finally arrived in the middle of June 1605, and then no more time was lost. Three days later, the 19th June, 1605, the search for a better site began. Although the explorers went further south than Cape Cod, to the waters of Nausett harbour, the place finally chosen was back in the Bay of Fundy, this time on its south shore. There on an inlet now known as Annapolis Basin they founded Port Royal, building that autumn a sturdy fort which had the added advantage of a good well within its walls. This was a much better location than Ste. Croix Island, and its selection really marks the foundation of Acadie. A most important aspect of its establishment was the attitude shown towards the project by the Indians around Port Royal. These were Micmac Indians, members of those tribes grouped together by contemporary anthropologists as representatives of the Eastern Woodland culture, the Malecite, Passamaquoddy, Penobscot, Abenaki, and Womenack, all connected by related Algonkian speech. They were not particularly numerous and the bands were very loosely connected with one another. Migratory hunters, fishers and food-gatherers, their interests in the lands through which the Acadians would spread did not bring

This reconstruction of Port Royal was made following the descriptions of Lescarbot and Champlain. It stands where the original was first built.

them into conflict with the latter. As a result, the Acadian villages could be, and were, built without much concern for questions of defence against the indigenous inhabitants. Indian skills were passed on to the immigrants, and occasionally an Indian woman would be absorbed into an Acadian village through marriage.* It was not until the eighteenth century that the Acadians had to cope with Indian attacks. During the seventeenth century the Acadian settlements would find their foes the English, the French, and, on one occasion, the Dutch.

In 1605, however, the colony had barely begun. European cultivation of the land had not yet started. After a much less harrowing winter than that of the previous year, the spring of 1606 once more brought an anxious period before the ships

*Two documented cases of this: one which sprang from quarrels over an estate, where it was necessary to prove marriage: B.N Nouv. Acq. Fr. 9281; and in Registre Paroissiale, Port Royal, I, (A.A.Q.) the marriage contract of Anne Roy, 1703, showed her to be half-Indian.

arrived from France. The pioneers still had not gathered enough knowledge of their new environment to permit them to build their lives the way they wished without continued support from their former homeland. They needed more people, as well as new materials, if their settlement was to flourish and become more than just a centre for trade and exploration. The ships finally arrived in July. Then there was a great celebration. A tun of wine was opened "so that some of them drank until their caps turned around."[4] On one of the ships was Marc Lescarbot, lawyer, who was to spend almost the rest of his life in Acadie and whose diaries have been a major source of information for the reconstruction of the life of its settlers during the seventeenth century. Once more, in 1606 as in 1605, renewed contact with France brought renewed energy to the pioneers. Vegetables were planted and Lescarbot noted in his diary that "farming must be our goal. That is the first mine for which we must search, and it is better worth than the treasures of Atahualpa: for whoso has corn, wine, cattle, linen, cloth, leather, iron and lastly, codfish, need have naught to do with treasure."[5]

By the spring of 1607 it looked as if the settlement was on the verge of being self-supporting. There is a tradition that one of the colonists who had arrived the year before, Louis Hebert, had brought his wife with him, and that she gave birth that spring to a daughter, who would be thus the first Acadian born.[6] In any case, so strong a sense of optimism pervaded the settlers then that cultivation began before the ships arrived from France. This time, however, the effort was in vain. The ships that came in May, 1607, brought the news that de Monts had had his privileges and charters revoked. This was a disastrous blow. Those who fitted out the expedition, de Monts and his companions, had financed it largely on credit. They had relied on a monopoly of the fur trade as a means of paying their debts. They had every interest in Acadie's development as a community but they had no money. In the late summer of 1607 the would-be settlers returned to France.

At least one family, however, was determined, in the words of Lescarbot, not to "abandon the beauties of this land, to say a lasting farewell to Port Royal."[7] This was the family of Jean de Biencourt, Sieur de Poutrincourt, who had come out with the first expedition of 1604. Although he too left in 1607, he managed to return in 1610. He found, to his delight, that the Indians had preserved Port Royal unspoilt. He was able to start sowing crops immediately, to refurbish for the winter, and to despatch his son, Charles de Biencourt, back to France with a good cargo of furs. Next spring, 1611, Madame de Poutrincourt came out with Charles. Once more it looked as if Acadie would be more than merely a name attached to an ill-defined area of North America, whose limits ran southeast of the St. Lawrence and northwest of Cape Cod. But within two years hopes were once more frustrated.

The first source of difficulties was the relationship of the Poutrincourt family with the religious and political power structure of seventeenth-century France. The original expedition of 1604 had been under Protestant leadership, although some of its most important members, including Poutrincourt himself, were Catholic. Neither de Monts nor Poutrincourt, however, demanded a particular religious belief from the people with whom they had political and economic dealings. On this they were in advance of their age, for the contemporary trend in France was towards a separation of Catholic and Protestant. The Edict of Nantes, which Henry IV had proclaimed in 1598 in order to settle the differences of religious opinion among his subjects, had established separate Protestant groupings within the structure of a Catholic state. It was less a measure that promoted a homogeneous treatment of all Frenchmen in political and social matters, irrespective of their religious allegiances, than one which put forward a "separate but equal" principle as a basis of religious toleration. In practical terms this meant not only a major division between Protestant and Catholic in France, important though this was, but also a host of tangled politics between various groups within these major divisions. Both Protestant and Catholic groups contained people dissatisfied with the conduct of the affairs of state, both had adherents who wished to see their opponents more rigorously confined and both had adherents desiring greater freedom of conscience for all. Poutrincourt found that this web of religious politics hampered not only his relations with the Protestant merchants of the Atlantic seaports, in particular with those of La Rochelle, but also affected his dealing with the Crown.

The assassination of Henry IV, in 1610, although its perpetrator was a poor lunatic killing from private griefs, embittered the religious question. Henry IV's widow, Marie de Medici, turned to the Jesuit order for support and counsel. Among the Catholics, the Jesuits at this time were the party whose zeal for their vision of God most often meant considerable earthly turmoil. In 1611 not only Madame de Poutrincourt came to Acadie but also two Jesuit fathers, Pierre Biard and Enemond Massé. The turmoil which these men entrained affected the relationship between Poutrincourt and the merchants of La Rochelle, the daily life of the establishment and also the relationship between Poutrincourt and the French court. La Rochelle was a major Protestant stronghold and the merchants were so disturbed at the idea of a Jesuit mission that they threatened to cut Poutrincourt's credit if the Jesuits became a dominant influence within the colony. The Jesuits themselves had but one idea in mind: missionary work among the Indians. Poutrincourt's heart was in the establishment of his community and the trading necessary for its flourishing. As a result there were clashes over what should be given most attention. The priests wanted not only contact with the Indians but contact of a particular type, and one which would emphasize the conversion to Catholicism rather than the exchange of guns for furs.

Further, by 1613, the Jesuit influence had managed to persuade the Crown of France to grant to the Marquise of Guercheville the right to colonise all of Acadie, save Poutrincourt's established seigneurie in the immediate neighbourhood of Port Royal. It was at this point that the internal question of who was to dominate Acadian affairs was suddenly and swiftly regulated by an outside influence. In July 1613, the Virginian pirate, Samuel Argall, swept up from Jamestown and sacked the small independent settlement which the Jesuits had achieved at St. Saveur as well as sacking and burning Port Royal itself. After this action, Acadie, as a European settlement, almost completely vanished until the end of the 1620's. But this obvious interruption to the growth of the colony did not completely eradicate the efforts of the years between 1604 and 1613. Men such as Charles Biencourt and Charles de St. Etienne de la Tour worked for Acadie even after this disaster and the ideas of the first pioneers were to prove, in many cases, strong enough to live until the colony was once more vigorously supported by

France. Thus some Acadian traditions can be traced to the earliest years of the colony.

From the outset the attempt to settle in Acadie was dominated by people who wished above all to build a new community for themselves in a new land. Although some members of the early expeditions wished to concentrate on the possible wealth to be gained from the fur trade, cultivation of the land held priority among the first who came to Acadie. At the same time, the wealth of the fisheries, especially those of the Atlantic coast, was explored. Fish was an alternative to the fur trade as a source of income, and the market for fish in Europe was steadier, if less glamorous, than that for fur. The settlement of Acadie was never the exploitation of one economic possibility, but was built upon the utilisation of all available resources.

Nor was it tied to any single political or ideological philosophy. The interest of the French monarchy in the affairs of Acadie was usually an interest at one remove: through the patent or charter delivered to the most successful of those asking for the right to colonise North America in the name of France. The valley of the St. Lawrence absorbed much more attention than Acadie, and the latter was always a subsidiary consideration to those governing France during the seventeenth century. As the century progressed, this had a great effect on the political life within the colony, which, at the local level, achieved a flexibility much greater than might have been expected. The settlement of the migrants owed much less to supervision by the central authority from France, and much more to their own initiative, than the official colonial policy of seventeenth-century France might approve. Yet a third trend established in these early years, which was to continue in later decades, was to be seen in the way in which the religious life of the colony was organised. Although the early expeditions were predominantly Catholic, they were not, as has been mentioned, predominantly missionary in outlook. The conversion of the local Indians to Catholicism was an important factor in Indian friendship for the pioneers, but such conversion was not the prime concern of the colony. The division between Jesuit and settler which occurred in the years 1610 to 1613 meant an independent activity by the latter among the Indians. As the seventeenth century continued, the colony knew other priests besides those of the Jesuit order, both for the servicing of Acadian religious needs and for those of the Indians. Catholicism in Acadie was much less homogeneous than might have been expected.

In sum, the traditions established in the colony before 1613 were, firstly, those of a mixed economy which included fur-trading, fishing and farming; secondly, friendship with the local Indians; thirdly, little precise instruction from France on the actual organisation and government of the community; and fourthly, the tradition of individual effort as opposed to action backed by the might of the court of France. As a result of this last, there was a greater tolerance for varying religious beliefs than was usual during the seventeenth century. The continuance of these traits after 1613 helped to build an Acadian community with a very distinctive character of its own. This character grew more interesting as other traditions evolved. These included not only the methods used to deal with the internal affairs of the Acadian villages, but also patterns of action to deal with French bureaucracy, and English officialdom, and the impact upon the colony of its North American neighbours, New England and New France.

As has already been noted, after 1613 attempts at establishing a self-supporting French settlement lapsed. Charles de Biencourt, Poutrincourt's son, continued as a fur-trader, and there is evidence that more than 25,000 pelts left Acadie for France in 1616. A Jesuit mission was intermittently maintained at the mouth of the St. John river, and fishing boats came to Chedabouctou. Then in 1621, James I of England and VI of Scotland granted to Sir William Alexander colonization rights over the area, which the charter in question called Nova Scotia, and which was located somewhere between the Gaspé and the Ste. Croix river.[8] This marks the appearance of yet another important aspect of Acadian history: the ability of both the French and the English governments to legislate the affairs of Acadie with little or no regard for what was actually happening in the area. However, there was no immediate battle between French and English groups bent on colonising the same land at the same time, because Sir William made no fruitful effort to develop his new charge until 1628. Then, with the help of the Kirke brothers, some seventy men and two women arrived to establish themselves at Port Royal.

These men, whose birthplace has never been satisfactorily determined, some authorities considering it to have been Dieppe, others in Scotland or England, were in the main professional pirates more or less working for England. They managed, among their other activities, to capture one Claude de la Tour who, with his son Charles, had taken over from de Biencourt fur-trading in Acadie.

The Kirke brothers took the elder, Claude de la Tour, to London, where he managed to obtain baronetcies for himself and his son. These were conferred in 1629 and 1630 respectively.[9] In 1613, Charles, the son, also obtained the commission of "Lieutenant-General of the French king" in Acadie.[10] Their recognition by two European courts was to prove of great value to the la Tour family. The provisions of the treaty of St. Germain-en-Laye, 1632, gave the colony to France, but later in the century the fortunes of war would make Acadie an English possession and Charles de la Tour would be recognised as its legal governor by Cromwell.

There has been considerable historical controversy over the probity of the la Tour family, and some historians have seen their actions as political opportunism of the worst sort. Evidence which shows something of their background is to be found in a letter to Cardinal Richelieu from Charles de la Tour. In it, Charles said that he had lived in Acadie since the age of fourteen and that he was then thirty-four.[11] During these twenty years, he wrote, he had lived as did the people of the country, hunting and fishing in their manner, wearing clothes of their style, and, with a small group of companions, existing without support from the French and in fear of the English. Was there no hope, he pleaded, for aid for the real development of a colony in this so beautiful land? This letter is dated 1627. For the la Tours, Acadie, rather than the France that they had left, was their chosen country, their homeland. Coming to her shores on the threshold of manhood, Charles gave to Acadie his energies and his intelligence and saw success for himself in terms of his position in this land rather than in honours elsewhere. The approbation of Europe being necessary to the development of Acadie, la Tour had to have continued connections with both France and England, but in the final analysis the land of his loyalty was Acadie. Many writers have assumed that the migrant must retain always a shaded longing for his original land and a final loyalty for old ties. This assumes a great deal about the society left behind and the migrant's position in it, as well as a great deal about the society to which the individual has come. There is no such imperative. Vibrant feelings for the new home can be more powerful than any memory. The essence of Acadian history is the development of such deep local attachments to their immediate realities, farms, ships, villages, kin, neighbours, that the political demands of both France and England became of minor, and almost insubstantial, account to the Acadian.

At the end of the 1620s, however, there was not yet an Acadian in existence, although Charles de la Tour may have been a close approximation. But the international position having been agreed upon, France now decided to establish her control in the area more firmly. A cousin of Cardinal Richelieu, Isaac de Razilly, was commissioned in 1632 to repatriate the settlers sent out by Sir William Alexander four years earlier, the late result of James I's initiative, and to people the colony with French settlers. The first part of the work was quickly completed, and to aid him with the second de Razilly chose a personal second-in-command, a relative named Charles de Menou d'Aulnay de Charnisay. Acadie now had in effect two lieutenant-governors, because the earlier commission to Charles de la Tour was not revoked. While de Razilly was alive, d'Aulnay* and la Tour were bound by his control, but when he died in 1635, they fought each other bitterly for the governorship of the colony. The duel lasted fifteen years. There were actual battles in Acadie, and at one point, la Tour asked for and received help against his rival from Massachusetts. Both men crossed the Atlantic to plead their case at the Court of France. D'Aulnay was at first the more successful in Europe, for the Queen Mother, acting in the name of Louis XIV, confirmed his rights over Acadie in 1647. But in 1650 the unhappy man was drowned when his canoe hit a sand-bank on the St. John river. La Tour immediately married the widow and had his right as "governor, and lieutenant general of all the lands, territories, shores and frontiers of Acadie"[12] confirmed in 1651. Despite the time,

---

*This is the usual method of referring to the man.

money, men and effort that had been involved in the duel, the colony which la Tour surveyed that year was in far better shape than it had been in 1632.

Firstly, there was actually a colony in existence. Some forty families were well established at Port Royal. The dyking of the sea marshes, a practice which was to become typically Acadian, had started. There were other smaller settlements in the colony, notably at La Have, and there were a fair number of single men present, too, soldiers and contract labourers working for a set term usually of three years. The fishing post at Chedabuctou Bay was flourishing as well. Secondly, the fact that the settlers ran their own affairs gave it great strength. The duel between d'Aulnay and la Tour had left the settlers brought from France almost without official organisation. There was a theoretical structure of command and d'Aulnay, in particular, made an effort to ensure that those who had come to Acadie under his aegis were supplied with goods from Europe and subject to his orders. But the families acted with considerable independence, opening up land without much regard for official registration of title. Many of the reports on life in this period are retrospective accounts, gathered in the 1670s, when Acadie, having survived one more English conquest, was being surveyed by France in order that the state of the colony should be discovered. The strongest impression to be gained from these reports is that the relationship between the families settling Acadie and the men who held in their hands commissions from the French court was very loose. The constant need of d'Aulnay and la Tour to pay more attention to each other than to the day-to-day activities of the settlements meant a gradual development, firstly of leaders among the settlers themselves, second-in-command to either la Tour or D'Aulnay but men with considerable power in the colony, and secondly, a casual attitude towards official demands. The latter would be met when required, but there was little sense of urgency. Men like Jean Theriot and Jacques Bourgois, both present in Acadie about 1635, signed in 1671 a declaration about the value of the work done in the colony by d'Aulnay,[13] and this declaration brings out strongly the lack of formality in the relationships of commissioned governors and governed, a lack of formality which was of considerable proportion when compared with the contemporary state of affairs in most rural areas of France.

Another aspect of daily life in the colony which gave it considerable strength was the family relationships, the kinship lines, of the settlers. Although the Acadians were not transplanted as a group from just one section of France, among these early settlers there were a fair number of people who had links with one another before they left Europe. Some nine or ten families were already related to one another by marriage before they left Europe. Jean Theriot, for example, was related to the Dupuis family by his sister, who had married Martin Dupuis: the evidence for such assertions coming from a comparison of French parish registers, passenger lists of the ships, and the Acadian nominal censuses.[14] Once settled in Acadie, links among the migrants were strengthened by the custom of marriages between the daughters of the early settlers and men who had originally thought to spend only a short time in the colony. The expansion of settlement was a growth of villages founded by people closely connected to the inhabitants of those first established. The newcomers to the colony did not become hived off into separate areas but were assimilated by those already established in Acadie. Such separation as did exist was between the officials, military or civil, French or English, and those wresting a livelihood from the new lands.

As to the actual growth of the Acadian population, from the very beginning this proved to be a story not only of fertility, but also of survival. When at the same time in France, as Goubert has discovered, the rates of infant mortality were commonly 28% of births, and of those born less than 50% reached the age of twenty-one,[15] the settlers of Acadie saw their children flourish, and families of ten and twelve all surviving to adulthood was the general pattern. Thus when la Tour's rule was challenged by the English in 1654 the colony, although small, and having been able to grow very little since 1651, was nevertheless tough enough to survive this new trial. The English raid captured Port Royal. The raiders had actually left Massachusetts to attack New Netherlands (New York). The declaration of peace between the English and the Dutch made the captains turn north instead of south. However, la Tour's commission, procured from Charles I, was recognised as valid by Cromwell and he was able to govern Acadie, firstly for his own benefit and after 1658 for Sir Thomas Temple, with whom he made a variety of agreements. Although between 1658 and 1670 the English were the sovereign power in Acadie, the day-to-day life of the colony was to remain basically French and to develop along the lines earlier established.

Acadie became officially French once more by the Treaty of Breda in 1667, although it was not until 1670 that the colony was actually handed over to France by Sir Thomas Temple. As has been noted, one of the first official acts of the new regime was to discover what was in existence, and the census that was carried out gave the colony about 350 inhabitants, a figure which is probably a little conservative. They included the Melanson brothers who, a later commentator mentions, were of Scottish ancestry and Roger Kuessy,* who in a legal matter in Quebec in 1685 affirmed that he was Irish by origin. The most important settlement was Port Royal, but there were other small establishments at Pubnico, Cap Neigre, Port Rochelais, Pentagouet and Musquodoboit, and even a family of six on Cape Breton Island. The census in most cases gives the names and ages of husband, wife and children, as well as their possessions. In two cases, however, Pierre Melanson and Etienne Robichaud, the census-taker was informed that his questions were not going to be answered. Most of the men were identified just as "laboureur", but this meant a man who had land and animals. The colony possessed people who considered themselves trained in various ways, the list going from the practice of surgery through carpentry, barrel-making, tailoring, masonry, and various branches of the lumber trade to blacksmith, armourer and candlemaker. From this basis, with the influx of around forty families brought out after 1671, the colony expanded during 1670-1686, going from approximately 375 in 1671 to approximately 515 in 1679, and over 800 in 1686.[16]

During these years Acadie usually had its own governor, but none of the governors managed to bring the colony into what they considered a satisfactory condition. Perrot, who was in command from 1684 to 1687, and who, in some ways, had con-

---

*The non-French origin of these men is also attested to in the legal records left in the eighteenth century by their descendants, and preserved in Vannes, Morbihan, France.

siderable sympathy with the achievements of the colonists, complained of the way the Acadians built their villages, all strung out in a long line instead of compactly assembled; of the way the young people left Port Royal to lead far too independent lives at places like Beaubassin; of the difficulty of surveying the activities of people who had such possibilities of "contacts with the Indians and the leading of an easy vagabondish and immoral life."[17] But Perrot noted how well the Acadians lived from the produce of the land, hunting, fishing and agriculture, how much they knew of woodcraft, and how efficient they were in building and using birch-bark canoes. The attitude of his successor, Louis-Alexandre des Friches de Meneval, who commanded the colony from 1687 to 1690, is a curious contrast: he agreed with all of Perrot's complaints but went further and saw in the colony only poverty, inefficiency and neglect. The birch-bark canoes, so admirably adapted to moving along the shores and into the small rivers, he saw only as not being as large as the French fishing vessels. He considered the methods of farming slothful and the Acadian clothing and furniture pitiful in the extreme. Perrot, on the other hand, had noted that the Acadians could feed themselves very well and that trades such as carpentry and masonry had been taught by one generation to the next.

This contemporary difference of opinion about the Acadians has been perpetuated by historians. The nineteenth-century American historian Francis Parkman characterised them as a poverty-stricken people who had "the social equality which can only exist in the humblest conditions of society."[18] But Emile Lauvrière, a French historian writing in the 1920s, saw them as dwelling in "une sorte de communisme spontané que seules rendaient possible l'abondance de leurs terres et la solidité de leurs vertus."[19] Like the reports of the two governors, the writers have produced different accounts by asking different questions. An American historian who wrote about Acadian history in the 1920s, John Bartlett Brebner, has suggested that there were two Acadies, the one of the international conference table and the one in which people lived. This idea of dichotomy can be further developed, for the Acadie of the international conference table was the Acadie that was a colony, a dependency of France, an area subjected to control by Europe, an area to be conquered by New Englanders in 1710, and a very weak part of the French empire indeed.

Parkman left his personal notes and papers to the Massachusetts Historical Society in Boston, and one can compare the sections he selected to copy from documents in Paris with the originals, either in the Bibliothèque National or in the Archives National in Paris. What impressed Parkman was that the Acadians possessed very few artifacts other than those smuggled to them by the Boston merchants, and that the French garrison, whether at Pentagoet or at Port Royal, was poorly outfitted and quite incapable of protecting the colony. Between 1690 and 1710 the colony was fairly constantly subject to English attacks of varying severity. Some attackers merely burnt and pillaged, like those on Chignecto in 1696 and on Chignecto and Minas in 1696 and 1704. Others were repulsed with moderate loss, like those on Port Royal after 1700 when the defenders set fire to the town the better to defend themselves. But two of them, the Phipps raid of 1690 and that of Nicholson and Vetch in 1710, were of much greater severity. The last, of course, meant the exit of Acadie from the French Empire and her entrance as Nova Scotia into the British, for the conquest was confirmed by the Treaty of Utrecht in 1713. The letters of the men sent to govern the Acadians during those years are detailed reports of the inadequacies of the colony's defence, the inroads made by the New Englanders, the amount of money Louis XIV ought to grant to Acadie so that it could be a French bastion of strength in North America. What is not mentioned by Parkman, and rarely stressed in the official despatches, is the other Acadie.

Throughout these years New England merchants smuggled goods to the Acadians, and also acted as the middlemen between them and the West Indies for Acadian purchases of rum and molasses. The Acadians were not the beneficiaries of a charitable enterprise. They paid for their purchases in agricultural products, furs, fish and a considerable amount of coinage. The French garrison and officials were paid in coinage and this went quickly into Acadian hands. On the very eve of the capture of the colony in 1710, Subercase, its last French-appointed governor, received a letter from Versaille saying: "Therefore, as you inform me that there is plenty of money in Acadie but the inhabitants do not put it into circulation, it is your business to discover means of getting it into circulation."[20] The demographic picture of the Acadians excludes any possibility of a major food shortage of long duration, for the impact of such, as Goubert has demonstrated, is an immediate check on growth. The scarcities referred to in official despatches were scarcities of particular substances rather than lack of all types of food. Between 1690 and 1710 the second Acadie survived without difficulty.

One of its strengths, of course, was its close-knit character. As has been noted, during the seventeenth century the new migrants to the colony were never in such great numbers as to swamp the original families, and each village was not only a related entity but was linked with the next. René Bernard, for example, moved from Port Royal to Beaubassin sometime during the 1680s and one of his sons went on to Grande-Pré. The family of the Irishman, whose name had by the end of the seventeenth century become Jean Cassey, spread themselves between Beaubassin and Grand-Pré. Leading citizens in one community had grandchildren married to each other in the next, and a raid on one village meant support for the victims from somewhere else in the colony. Each village knew the affairs of the other, not only as part of the same community at large, but through a network of aunts, cousins, parents, children, in-laws, uncles and nephews. What was being developed by the Acadians after 1670 was a clan, a body of people united by blood ties, common beliefs and common aims for the group as a whole, and this meant that they flourished despite the lack of a uniform and stable direction from a financially influential headquarters. Thus by 1710 the Acadians were a community which showed the way in which the settlers and their descendants had responded firstly to the demands of the lands on which they lived, secondly to the impact upon them of the relationships among themselves, and thirdly to the implementation of policies determined elsewhere but which affected them deeply. These interlocking circumstances were moulded by the events of the seventeenth century to produce at its end what had not existed at its start: a people called Acadian.

Chapter II

Acadian Politics: 1710-1748

The arguments over the Acadian standard of living at the end of the seventeenth century pale before those over their history during the eighteenth century. Although the most bitter debates surround the deportation itself and centre on the seventeen-fifties, the situation of 1710 to 1713 is also much discussed. By 1970 more than three hundred books and articles had been published about the Acadians, and many of them opened with a description of what exactly had come under British control by the terms of the Treaty of Utrecht in 1713, for the boundaries of the colony, referred to in the document as "Acadie or Nova Scotia", were nowhere precisely delineated. This meant considerable trouble as time went on, for if the colony was now British the French still held considerable territory in the immediate neighbourhood: Isle Breton (Cape Breton Island), Isle St. Jean (Prince Edward Island). Further, the French claimed, sometimes garrisoned, and were frequently the stronger military presence in the forests of what is now New Brunswick. Brebner, the American historian mentioned in the previous chapter, whose important work on the diplomatic aspects of Acadian history is as readable as it is scholarly, called the colony "a continental cornice" and wrote that "whatever (the) boundaries were, the important consideration was that any Acadie or any Nova Scotia lay inside the angle between the St. Lawrence route to French Canada and the northern route to New England which branched off from it south of Newfoundland."[1] The eighteenth century was to see the rapid development of English and French expansion in North America and, to quote from Brebner again, "what happened was that the English, pushing north and west, were directly opposed by the southerly and easterly thrust of the French, and something like an intermittent battlefront moved backwards and forwards between them. The fixed pivot on which the motion hinged was Nova Scotia, captured by the English in 1710, and held continuously until the end of the struggle."[2] To put it simply, the events of 1710 to 1713 opened a period in which the Acadians were to find their lands a border territory, and a territory which was to become of greater and greater strategic value as the years passed.

Arguments also sprang up, both during the eighteenth century and later, about the conditions under which the Acadians became part of the British Empire. The clauses of the Treaty of Utrecht which dealt with the Acadians as such, gave them "liberty to remove themselves within a year to any other place, as they shall think fit, together with all their moveable effects." If any decided to remain, they were to "be subject to the Kingdom of Great Britain" and "to enjoy the free exercise of their religion, according to the usage of the Church of Rome, as far as the laws of Britain allow the same."[3] These provisions were reinforced by a letter from Queen Anne to the officials administering the colony in 1713. Dated June 23rd of that year, it reads in part: "We . . . Signifie Our Will and Pleasure to you that you permit and allow such of them as have any lands . . . in the Places under your Government in Acadie . . . and are willing to Continue our Subjects, to retain and Enjoy their said Lands and Tenements without any Lett or Molestation as fully and freely as our other Subjects do . . . ."[4] The ambiguities in these provisions are manifold. The amount of freedom granted Roman Catholics by the laws of Great Britain, at the opening of the eighteenth century, was small and specifically excluded political rights. The limit set for the period of time during which the Acadians were to be allowed to sell their goods and emigrate was as imprecisely stated as the boundaries had been imprecisely drawn: a year from when? it was asked. Some historians consider a year from 1713 had been given, others that no limit had been placed, and it has been suggested that in constitutional law the Acadians' right to emigrate could not have been abrogated at any point. The apparently simple terms for the changeover of the colony in 1713 provide, therefore, considerable problems. But one thing emerges clearly from any study of the diplomatic correspondence about the provisions of Utrecht: the French government of Louis XIV tried every means in its power to hold on to the colony, and the government of Queen Anne was determined to take over "Nova Scotia or Acadie".

In 1713, the latter was successful, but the Acadians were by no means convinced that the last word had been said on the matter. As has been noted, France retained considerable territory close at hand and the Acadians were well aware of her power in the St. Lawrence valley. Nor was there any immediate evidence available to the Acadians to suggest that this conquest would be any more lasting than those the British had made before. Several Acadians were old enough to remember not only the Phipps raid, twenty years earlier, but the time of Temple. The colony had, in fact, been captured by the British on ten different occasions during the seventeenth century, and in any case, what did defeat really mean to the people of Acadie? In 1710, the man left in command at Port Royal, soon to be generally known as Annapolis Royal, had some five hundred assorted troops at his disposal to enforce his wishes over a population of more than two thousand five hundred, scattered along the shores of the Bay of Fundy and into the valley of the Peticodiac. As the years went by, the number of troops would diminish and the number of Acadians would increase. If the Acadians had been ruled by an efficient, autocratic regime under the French, the changeover might have meant more of an upheaval. But the evidence of the seventeenth century shows clearly that the Acadians, if not quite the "bunch of Republicans"[5] they appeared to Perrot, were an independent-minded people, and they regulated a considerable amount of their day-to-day affairs themselves, with little recourse to the transients sent to govern or garrison their lands.

The Acadians have frequently been characterised as an essentially "rural" people, and as having a general uniformity of personality best conveyed with phrases such as "simple farmers", "shrewd peasants", "devout people", and "innocent inhabitants of a Golden Age".* In reality they were as compli-

*The reader might like to compare the descriptions given by two Americans, Brebner, New England Outpost, pp. 204-5 and Gipson, The British Empire Before the Revolution, V 168-9, two Frenchmen, Rameau de St. Père, L'Acadie — Une colonie Féodale, chap. IV and Emile Lauvrière, La Tragédie d'une peuple, p. 81, and two Canadians, Frègault. La Guerre de la Conquête, p. 32 and Doughty, The Acadian Exiles, pp. 88-113 passim. The similtarity is striking as regards the theme of uncomplicated rural people whether the final character is seen as laudable or not.

38137

cated and as varied a group of humans as any other such society. From the settlers themselves there were men who rose to be militia captains after arriving in the colony as "laboureurs". Michel Boudrot, who came to Acadie as a "laboureur," ended as one of the most important officials of Port Royal. The arrangements of the Acadians' villages were decided by their wants and not by the demands of official authorities. None of them had any hestitation in carrying disputes from Acadie to France, to plead the rights of children born to marriage with an Indian woman, or to verify the boundaries of the land they had cultivated. The official correspondence of the French authorities in Acadie notes such cases with no expression of astonishment. Further, the Acadians looked upon the ecclesiastical authority with as critical an eye as they viewed the secular. Perhaps the most striking case of this, though by no means the only one, began in 1693 when the villagers of Beaubassin complained that their curé was far too intent upon missionary work among the Indians and paid far too little attention to work among the Acadians. The outcome was an apology from the curé to the village and a promise from the bishop of Quebec to rectify a situation whereby several Acadian settlements had been left without a priest for most of the year.

The Acadian was much more than just a seventeenth-century Frenchman living abroad. His style of living had produced methods of handling community affairs which had little in common with the ways of his cousins in Europe. Further, there was considerable English influence in the colony. The admixture of English people was small, but their impact was liable to be greater than their numbers since some of the families sprang from the Melanson brothers who were powerful landowners. The major source of English influence was an economic one. Over and over again the continuing trade between Acadie and New England is referred to in the despatches sent to France. One French official wrote, sympathetically enough: "It is not surprising that the Acadians lean towards the English, for they rarely hear talk of France nor receive her help, but are brought the necessities each year by the English."[6] This was in 1686 and there was no halt to the trade in axes and iron pots over the next twenty-four years. For the Acadians, the economy of their lives needed the connection with New England, a connection which, after all, had existed since the aid given to la Tour in the 1640s. As a result of these factors, the Acadian by 1710 was convinced not only of the need to speak for the colony, but of his right so to do. He evolved a policy which was based on his realisation of the position of the Acadian people as a border people, and of himself as the inhabitant of a land coveted by two powerful neighbours.

Essentially the Acadians' strategy was neutrality, for in their view, neither France nor England could be guaranteed as the final victor. Allegiance to the English was perfectly acceptable as long as it did not involve bearing arms against the French. Four years after the official British takeover of the colony, the Acadians worked out what they considered to be the terms on which they would remain under British government. In a letter dated 10th February, 1717, and sent to the officials at Annapolis Royal, the following points were made:

1. Acadian adherence to Catholicism must be respected;
2. The British officials must recognise that Acadians live with-in Indian territory, that the Indians are completely loyal to the French, that the Acadians would suffer Indian attacks should they openly align themselves in military matters against the French;
3. Acadians were a people with a history which ought to be taken into consideration by those attempting to govern them.

" . . . pendant que nos ancêstres ont été sous la Domination angloise on ne leur Jamais exigé de pareille Serment"[7] ran the letter: explicit swearing of a total commitment to the English was refused. "Look back to the last time you ruled us," the village elders said, "what was wrong with that arrangement?" This essential belief in their own right to argue their destiny comes out even more strongly in another Acadian letter of the same year which states that, while they would swear no oath, the Acadians would undertake with pleasure and gratitude not to initiate any design against his Britannic Majesty while they remained in Acadie.

Unfortunately for the Acadians, no one else was to consider the matter in this light. The attitude in Europe towards colonies at the opening of the eighteenth century was that they were the possession, in a very real sense indeed, of the European country to which they were, by international agreement, connected. As far as the colony was concerned, the degree of control actually exercised over its affairs was often more theoretical than practical. When the Treaty of Utrecht granted Britain "Acadie or Nova Scotia" in 1713, that power was still a rural island with a smallish population and a ramshackle system of government. At that time England and Wales had approximately six million people between them, though today the same area holds more than fifty millions. In 1713, the sole city was London with 674,000 inhabitants; in 1970 there were nine million Londoners. Travel on land in the eighteenth century was mostly by horse over appalling roads: London to Edinburgh was said to take ten days in summer and twelve in winter; by car today it takes about ten hours. And this slow speed was not only the speed of goods and people but also the speed of information, there being, of course, neither a telephone nor a telegraph system. Most problems which today come under some sort of surveillance from the central governments of a state were at that time dealt with at the local level. "Red tape" was minimal.

It was possible for two Secretaries of State to be in charge of all foreign and domestic affairs except taxation, and be the final authority for Scotland, Ireland, the Colonies, and the Army and Navy. In 1726 their entire staff numbered twenty-four. Minute surveillance of colonial affairs from London was a practical impossibility. Basically, the officials who worked for the established order, whether in France or in England, whether appointed or elected, dealt only with the most immediate, pressing and urgent questions. Imperial matters took their chance among other matters of state, and even when a particular colony was considered vital, the work of those in Europe was subject to modification by forces beyond their control, in particular the length of time it took to communicate anything across the Atlantic, whether it be knowledge, or money, or military force. The Acadians were by no means unrealistic in their pursuit of independence for, in fact if not in theory, they had been left alone by both France and England in the past, and could expect to enjoy a similar fate in the future. Further, for a considerable time this policy would prove to be successful.

In 1713, the most urgent problem for the British officials in Nova Scotia was the possibility of the Acadians' taking advantage of the permission given them to depart, coupled with the problem of how to govern them if they remained. Should they depart, Nova Scotia would be greatly impoverished and the nearby French territory of Isle Royale greatly strengthened. The French officials of Isle Royale were most anxious for the Acadians to come to them and when, by 1717, it was apparent that the Acadians were not going to do so, the governor wrote that he had always considered that the Acadians would become an essential part of the structure of Isle Royale and their refusal so to do made the situation very different. The Acadian decision not to emigrate has been much debated by historians. Did the British trick the Acadians into remaining? One of the twentieth-century historians, Emile Lauvrière, was convinced that they did. A French-Canadian historian, however, himself of Acadian descent, Antoine Bernard, concluded that the Acadians had absolutely no wish to go: "les Acadiens ne bougeront pas," he wrote.[8] Such a conclusion has much contemporary evidence in its favour, including a report by a Frenchman, the captain of a ship which visited Annapolis Royal in 1714, who wrote that the Acadians had no wish at all to quit their lands and comfortable houses for the hard work of establishing themselves anew on less inviting soil.

In considering the situation during these early years of British rule, it is essential to realise how little an impact that rule made on the day-to-day life of the Acadian villages. During the early months of the occupation, the winter of 1710 to 1711, Samuel Vetch, the man left in charge after the defeat of Subercase, began the practice which all later English officials followed, of dealing with the Acadians mainly by means of delegates they sent to him from each of the villages. This reduced the occasions of conflict, since the presence of the English in the colony was, to a very considerable extent, centred upon Annapolis Royal. The Acadians would be hard put to realise immediately what being a colony within the British Empire, rather than the French Empire, would mean. They spent their time and energies as they had always done: in developing their lands, hunting, fishing, expanding their families, and trading and smuggling. Previously, commerce with New England had been smuggling, that with Ile Royale, trade. The situation was now more or less precisely reversed. The establishment of the great grey fortress of Louisbourg on the southern coast of Ile Royale provided the Acadians with an expanding market, which they shared with Boston. In effect, there was little under the new regime to perturb the Acadians except the matter of the oath of allegiance, and even this was settled to Acadian satisfaction by 1730.

Vetch had struggled between 1710 and 1713 without success to make the Acadians take an oath of loyalty to Queen Anne, and the officials who succeeded him inherited his problem. What was to be done with a disobedient Acadian? Vetch himself counselled against deportation, since the obvious destination for the Acadian in his view would be French territory. Moreover, the disobedience was a complex reaction: not all Acadians reacted in the same way to the same oath, and there

Oath offered to the Acadians: this copy of the original document was made by Dr. Andrew Brown in 1791. The words in English are his notes.

were no signs of rebellion against British rule other than a refusal to comply without argument to the demand for the oath of allegiance. It is worthwhile stressing this point: many Acadian villages returned an oath of their own composition to the British authorities, swearing loyalty to the British Crown, providing that their religious beliefs were respected and they should never be required to bear arms against French or Indian. As the years passed, certain officials, notably Governor Philipps, who was governor of Nova Scotia from 1717 until 1749, and a much less powerful man, Ensign Wroth, considered that an oath with these provisions was preferable to no oath at all. As a result, by 1730 the Acadians had every reason to believe that they had managed to bring the British authorities to agree to their terms for remaining in Nova Scotia. Unfortunately, the authorities in London did not see the matter in the same light.

Considering the tremendous debates that exist over what oath was offered, what was taken, and what the legal and constitutional position of the Acadians was in 1755, it is worthwhile examining the grounds for the Acadian belief that they had made their position clear. For Governor Philipps did not report to London the reservation which other documentation shows the Acadians believed had been accorded to them. In the colony itself Acadian neutrality was taken as stated by later officials, even if they did not consider it to be desirable. Paul Mascerene, the Huguenot who was to become the lieutenant-governor of Nova Scotia during one of its most troubled periods, the 1740s, and whose mother tongue had been French, so that there is no question of his ability to understand the Acadian, wrote in 1748: "Although the reservation not to take up arms was not inserted by Philipps in 1730, the French always maintained that this promise had been given them, and I understand from those who were at Minas for the taking of the Oath that indeed such a promise had been granted them."[9] Secondly, in the petitions of the Acadians in exile to the colonial governments whose charge they were, in Pennsylvania for example, the fact that they had been promised their neutrality by Ensign Wroth was stated frequently. Thirdly, as Brebner has pointed out, "thereafter 1730 most Englishmen spoke of them as 'the Neutrals' or 'the neutral French'."[10] Finally, the curés of Grande-Pré and Pisiquid drew up a document immediately after the occasion of

Phillips' visit to the effect that the settlers had been exempted from bearing arms and fighting in war against either French or Indian, a document which they despatched to the government of France. The Acadians had considerable grounds for believing that they had successfully established their position.

Unfortunately neither French nor English, whether the governments of London or Paris, Quebec or Boston, agreed with this view. Firstly, no credence at all was given by them to the Acadian belief that it was their own right to establish the terms of their political lives, and secondly, the Acadian independence from France was not recognised either by the French or the English. While the situation remained peaceful, these matters remained without much importance for the Acadian, but the arrival of Anglo-French hostilities would bring them out into the open.

This position of neutrality was the Acadian's adjustment to the conditions of political life with which he was faced, not merely a passive stand. The English had little military strength in the colony. Until the arrival of Cornwallis in 1749 the number of troops garrisoning Nova Scotia was barely two hundred; by the same date the number of Acadians in Nova Scotia had grown to over seven thousand. There were no English settlements within Nova Scotia, other than Annapolis Royal, of any significance whatsoever, before 1749. The French were careful not to provoke open war, but their new fortress of Louisbourg, which had been built during the 1720s, was not to be ignored. The Indians were in the woods that surrounded the Acadian villages and clashes between English and Indian were an ever-present reminder to the Acadians of the strength of the latter and the weakness of the former. The Acadian policy was an attempt to emerge with an independent stand which would not bankrupt their credit with either France or England. Their manner of swearing allegiance to the British Crown was their expression of this.

The Acadians' neutrality was severely tested when war came to the colony in 1744. It was during this period that events reached such a level of ambiguity that the Acadians could look back on it and see it as a time when they proved their loyalty to the English Crown beyond a shadow of a doubt, and New Englanders could consider that the exact opposite had been

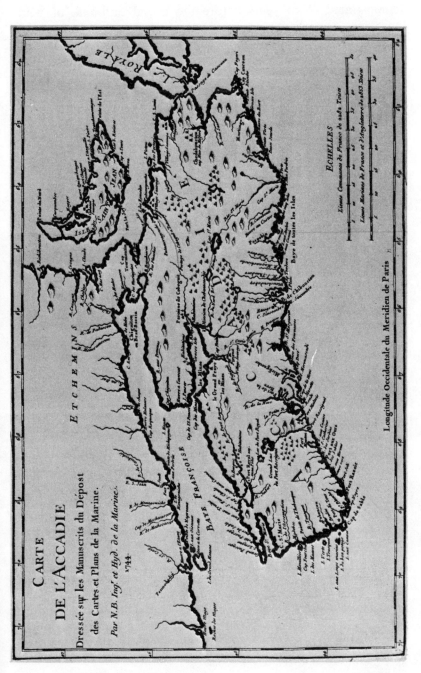

Map of Acadia by Jacques-Nicolas Bellin (1703-1772) from *Histoire de la Nouvelle-France*, Vol. 1, by L. P. Charlevoix.

demonstrated. Two years before the actual outbreak of war, Mascerene, then lieutenant-governor of the colony, wrote to the Duke of Newcastle that "the frequent rumours we have had of War being declared against France, have not as yet made any alteration in the Temper of the Inhabitants of this Province, who appear in a good disposition of keeping to their oaths of fidelity."[11] Mascerene was not deceived when war finally came in 1744. On June 9th he reported to Governor Philipps that he had done all in his power to "keep the French inhabitants in their fidelity, who promise fair and yet assist us in repairing our breaches."[12] On the same day he wrote to the Board of Trade, saying that the French inhabitants had given him assurances that they would maintain their "fidelity to his Majesty which they seem to testifie in having given their assistance in the works going on for the repairs of this Fort."[13] At the end of the month Mascerene wrote to Governor Shirley of Massachusetts to inform him of the general situation. His letter gives a concise summary of the Acadians' position.

July 28th, 1744.

The French Inhabitants as soon as the Indians withdraw from us brought us Provisions and continue to testifie their resolution to keep to their fidelity as long as we keep this Fort. Two Deputies arriv'd yesterday from Minas, who have brot me a Paper containing an association sign'd by most of the Inhabitants of that place to prevent Cattle being transported to Louisbourg according to the Prohibition sent them from thence. The French Inhabitants are certainly in a very perillous Situation, those who pretend to be their Friends and old Masters having let loose a parcel of Banditti to plunder them, whilst on the other hand they see themselves threatened with ruin and Destruction if they fail in their allegiance to the British government.[14]

Throughout Mascerene's term of office the Acadians maintained their shaky neutrality. Even when New England's capture of Louisbourg, in 1745, released the frightened reaction of the Canadians on to their unfortunate heads, Mascerene found himself able to testify that the Acadians "refused to bear arms, even on behalf of France, even in the presence of French troops." "The generality of the inhabitants of this province," he wrote, "possess still the same fidelity they have done before, in which I endeavour to encourage them."[15] As with the question of the limits of Acadie, of the conditions of cession, and of the oath itself, historians have argued over the position of the Acadians during these years, and many have agreed with contemporaries of Mascerene that the latter drew too rosy a picture. A nineteenth-century Canadian, Archibald, assembled evidence to show that "in every hostile enterprise against the Province, some of their number (the Acadians) took part in the fray and always on the side of the enemy."[16] He did not invent his evidence.

What controls the conclusions of both Mascerene and the historian is the aim of the account which they write. Archibald is interested in the political history of the British Empire, and in the strength of the British position. For him, it is above all the story of ruler and ruled. For Mascerene, the problems of daily administration are paramount. He is writing to London to inform them of the local temper of what he sees he has to control. Neither is interested in an exhaustive reconstruction of Nova Scotian or Acadian history, and both tend to see the Acadians linked with something more important than themselves. It is not really surprising that the existence of an Acadian policy has been given such little consideration. Constitutionally they belonged to British rule and in matters of religion to the control of France. There has been a great deal of evidence left by both these powers about their relations with the Acadians, and the documents left by the Acadians themselves are few and far between. However, an interesting picture of Acadian life emerges when, instead of asking whether the Acadians were loyal to the French or to the English, questions are asked about the extent to which British officialdom entered into the daily life of the Acadian villages and the amount of contact on a daily level between Acadian village and British power. Similar questions asked about the contact between Acadian and French priest and about the actual as opposed to the theoretical dominance of Catholicism in Acadian affairs further amplify the picture of the Acadians as ordinary human beings, not mere puppets. As has been suggested earlier, Acadians conducted many of their affairs themselves and were themselves the determinant for many of their traditions. The idea that what was left outside British control came under French supervision ignores a wide area of Acadian experience.

In particular, such a viewpoint ignores the root of Acadian life: the way in which they settled their lands. The very position of the villages within the peninsula gave their inhabitants considerable independence. The major settlements were a hundred miles or more from the centre of official government, Annapolis Royal, where the English were established. Even the French officials had complained of the difficulty of supervising these same settlements: in the 1690s, the French lieutenant-governor had between eighty and one hundred and twenty men to garrison a population of approximately two thousand in the 1740s, the English lieutenant-governor had approximately two hundred men to garrison a population of over seven thousand. In both cases, the result was the same: an inability to control Acadian development of the land. Writing in 1740, Mascerene stated "many of the Acadians . . . look out for land and . . . make settlements there contrary to the orders often repeated to restrain them."[17] Nor did the position of the villages merely affect the political development of the Acadians; it also had an impact upon their religious activities. A survey of the colony for the purposes of religion, undertaken for the Bishop of Quebec in 1737, suggested that the size of the population and its scattered situation (for the villages were not only distant from Annapolis Royal but often quite far from each other) necessitated at least six priests permanently resident within Nova Scotia.[18] This figure was never attained. Although some settlements had a resident priest for several years, many had only an itinerant one, and the parish registers show that often baptisms and marriages were blessed in groups, a common occurrence where priests visit, rather than reside in, the parish. The impact of priestly authority is always difficult to calculate, however, and much depends on the man who holds the office. The Acadian attitude to both religion and politics needs to be placed in the context of their daily life.

The Acadians were first and foremost a family people. The demographic development had been such that the original settlers and their descendants absorbed each new group of migrants into their community. The new families which came to Acadie after 1671 were quickly joined to the original settlers and did not form separate enclaves. The expansion of the colony, as has been suggested, was an expansion from a centre of settlement, and each new village was linked to one previously established by family ties. The natural increase of the Acadians was evidence of remarkable fertility, for it approached the quadrupling of the population every thirty-six years. From 1710 the arrival of new migrants among the Acadians fell to practically nothing, but by 1748 the population had grown from two thousand five hundred to nearly eight thousand.[19] In terms of everyday life this population growth meant a community of multi-family households, to use the term which the American geographer Clark has chosen. His work on the development of the Acadians has concentrated on their use of the economic possibilities of the colony and is a most scholarly compilation of data about Acadian economic life. The Acadians usually lived as members of households which contained three or four generations. Not only was infant mortality extremely low; Acadians lived long, and septuagenarians were common. The economic structure of the Acadians meant for the women a preoccupation with spinning, weaving, dyeing, knitting and sewing, to produce clothes; with preserving and cooking, with gardening, and with the day-to-day surveillance of the very young and the very old. For the men it meant farming and fishing, hunting and building, tool-making and carpentry in order to provide basic foods, shelter and furniture. Clark's work provides ample evidence of how well this division of labour worked. Life among the Acadians, from 1710 to the end of the 1740s, was life within a successful agricultural society.

Gunnar Myrdal, the Swedish economist, has observed that in discussing agricultural societies one must examine not only the type of land farmed and the density of population in a particular area but also how many people from the population are needed to produce that particular level of subsistence from that land. Among the Acadians, the level of subsistence produced was high and in most years a marketable export was available. The land was used extensively, that is to say the villagers spread their dwellings out around bays and through valleys, avoiding in the eighteenth century, as they had in the seventeenth century, the clearing of the forested uplands. The production of necessities under their system employed the labour available, and all commentators are agreed that the pattern of Acadian life was industrious. Any examination of the Acadians as families, as people facing the problems of what could be eaten in winter, of how the children were to be clad, produces the response: by the work of the Acadians themselves. An examination of eighteenth century records of ships sailing to and from Nova Scotia, while far from complete, shows how little the Acadians depended upon the rest of the world for necessities. What they received were various forms of alcohol, mostly by way of Louisbourg from France but also by way of Boston from the Caribbean; iron tools and cooking pots, mainly from Boston; blankets from Boston and linens from Louisbourg; and a variety of other goods such as nails and molasses from both sources.

One of the most interesting records from this period is to be found in the commercial records of the French, and allows a comparison of Acadian and New England trade with Louisbourg in 1740.[20] The value of the New England trade was much greater than that of the Acadians, and included bricks and planks, furniture and saws. The Acadians took to Louisbourg chickens and pigs, flour and cod, eels and hay, a variety of furs, and other goods of this sort. Their ships sailed from Beaubassin, Tatmegouche, Baie Verte, Chebouctou, Minas, Cap de Sable and Annapolis Royal itself. In all there were sixteen ships involved in this particular trade in 1740, and they ranged in size from the eight-ton *Hazardeau* with a cargo of ten assorted furs, moose, bear and otter, flour, peas, as well as feathers for the feather beds, to the thirty-ton *Charles,* which carried thirty-six live steers. The total value of this particular line of Acadian export came to just under 27,000 livres, and that of the New England trade for the same year, according to the same source, to 49,147 livres.* This record, of course, is incomplete: details can be found of Acadian exports to other destinations, including New England. The major importance of this document lies less in its details of a particular movement of particular goods, than in its indication of a more varied life for the Acadians than

*The approximate value of the **livre** in today's money would be $7.

would otherwise be suspected. Like the records of a Marseilles proposal for a hat factory in Acadie in the 1690s, of a complaint of a ships' captain that he was unable to complete the carrying of coal from Acadie to Rochfort in the 1680s, of the diary of a Boston merchant aboard a ship trading in coal with Minas in the 1730s, these documents have much in common with the documents used by medieval historians. They are clues whose final interpretation provides much matter for disagreement and whose final utility depends on how well they are assembled together and considered in relation to many other factors.

This parallel between Acadian history and medieval studies can be carried a little further, for the great lack in Acadian history, as in medieval, is personal memoirs. In reconstructing Acadian life during the early decades of the eighteenth century, one can consult the official reports of the English, and in some cases their personal letters and papers as well; there are also similar records of the French, the priests, the authorities at Louisbourg and Quebec. But so far, few personal documents by the Acadians for the period before 1755 have come to light. There do exist, of course, some general letters from the Acadians to higher officials, both French and English. But these are the work and expression of a group, more in the nature of petition and remonstrance than of personal commentary. In the main, estimation of Acadian beliefs and ideas, like the estimation of many categories of human experience during the Middle Ages, rests to a very considerable extent on the evaluation of other contemporaries and on the analysis of institutional records. Acadian relations with the British are revealed to a very large extent through the reports of officials, not from Acadian statements, and Acadian religious attitudes are to be deduced from the reports of priest to bishop and not from Acadian testimony.

Despite the limitations of the source material available, certain areas of Acadian experience before 1755 can be fairly completely reconstructed. To return to the question of their loyalty during the Anglo-French battles of the 1740s, much can be learnt of the Acadian political beliefs from their petitions. To Mascerene they wrote in 1742 that they were determined not to take up arms for or against Great Britain, implying thereby that they had the right to make a choice in the matter and that their chosen path was neutrality.[21] Two years later, they informed the Canadian soldiers who came among them that they had no intention of rising in revolt, for the government of England was bearable and all the incursions by the French meant merely death and destruction.[22] Such petitions have sometimes been dismissed by historians as being the work of Acadians who had no will of their own, but signed names or "x" to documents drawn up by their priests. The complementary views expressed by the two documents quoted above would mean that such a priest would be one who sympathised entirely with the Acadian wish to place loyalty to his community above loyalty to language and religion. In fact, such a criticism of these documents is an unnecessary complication. The whole history of the Acadians provides a simpler explanation: actions of self-confident people working toward the envisaged end of their own independence.

The experiences of the Acadians in exile, about which there is very much more documentation, and during which many Acadians put down their memories of the years before 1755, reveals a tremendous cohesion among them, as well as the existence of their own leaders. The system of deputies, already mentioned, is only one sign of the existence of such cohesion before 1755. By 1748 Nova Scotia was a British colony whose subjects lived with a great measure of local autonomy. Bound together by marriage, family connections provided social cohesion. Bound by economic necessity to produce their livelihood from their surroundings, they reaped an intimate acquaintance with the hills they hunted, the meadows they dyked, the waves they fished and the valleys they harvested. The Acadians lived in surroundings of considerable beauty which yielded them a comfortable supply of the necessities of life. From the record of their exile, which will be presented more fully in Chapter V, it is undeniable that the Acadians made considerable efforts to return to these lands from wherever they had been sent, whether they arrived in England or France, in Quebec, or further south on the American continent. Assimilation among aliens took place extremely slowly, if at all.

In sum, the Acadians displayed the traditional loyalties of a rural people, as described by Sir Lewis Namier: pride of place goes to the land cultivated, a certain affection to the most immediate and inescapable political centre, and a very minor emotion towards most physically distant powers, religious or secular. One of the French officials in 1751 said that the Acadian troubles sprang from too great an attachment to their lands. In his view, and he was one of the officers responsible for French policy towards the Acadians, these people had no right to decide their own hierarchy of values.[23] Of necessity, they were French. Similarly, the English governor in 1749 informed the Acadians that the question of their independence had been regulated once and for all by the Treaty of Utrecht: they had no choice but to live as perfect subjects of the King of England.[24] In 1748, the Acadians considered themselves Acadian, the French considered them unreliable allies, and the English, unsatisfactory citizens. During the next seven years these attitudes directed the policies of the parties concerned to the events which occurred; the result was the deportation of the Acadians.

Chapter III

Prologue to Disaster: 1749-1755

In 1749 the Acadians could look with considerable satisfaction on the results of their tactics. War had been fought through their lands and they had survived with few casualties and without irrevocably compromising their position with either the French or the English. Their behaviour had much in common with that employed by the tribes of the North West frontier of India

View of Halifax from Georges Island, 1749.

during the nineteenth century: the majority of people within the villages would initiate no revolt and would attempt to comply with the demands of the English, but some of the young men, their numbers always difficult to estimate, would join "their cousins over the border" in raiding the English soldiery.

38

Pathan or Acadian, neither would wholeheartedly help those who came to "free" them, less from attachment to the English than from a profound, and completely understandable, dislike of having their lands made into a battleground. Through Acadian eyes, the period 1710 to 1748 could be seen as one of considerable success: their population had steadily increased, and the political structure of the European empire of which they formed part had not seriously discommoded their development of their settlements according to their own wishes. The future might appear to be uncertain, but the past success of neutrality as a policy gave them confidence in its value as a tactic for the future. That such was the Acadian position can be seen in their attitude to Edward Cornwallis, the new governor who arrived in Nova Scotia in 1749. It was, however, a position based upon a serious misjudgement: that of concluding that the after-effects of the recent war and of the treaty of Aix-la-Chapelle would be negligible for them. In essence this treaty marks the end of the era in which Nova Scotia and her inhabitants were considered of minor importance by those making the imperial policies of France and England. The intensive consideration which the colony was about to receive would not last, but it would be of sufficient duration to alter profoundly the existence of the Acadians. As far as the English were concerned, this was partly due to the return of Louisbourg to the French and the consequent necessity for the policy-makers of London to pacify the New Englanders. This great fortress had been captured by New England troops and its surrender at the peace table infuriated them. Governor Shirley of Massachusetts, who had taken a considerable part in the negotiations of Aix-la-Chapelle, fighting hard for the retention of the fortress, now renewed his demands for a policy from the Lords of Trade which would make Nova Scotia a proper counter-balance to Louisbourg, and a strong outpost of English force. Partly because of his representations, partly from their own convictions that the problem of Nova Scotia was the most important point to "be determined for settling the same Tranquillity in America as has been so happily established in Europe",[1] the Lords of Trade set about the matter, and gave the colony an attention which it had never before received from the government in London.

Edward Cornwallis, thirty-six years old, twin brother of a future Archbishop of Canterbury, uncle of the Lord Cornwallis who was to surrender at Yorktown, was appointed captain-general and governor of the colony. He was armed with detailed plans to make the Acadians completely trustworthy subjects, to populate the colony with new Protestant immigrants and to replace Annapolis Royal with a new military and administrative centre.[2] He held his first Council meeting on board the "Beaufort" as it swung on the tides in Chedebucto Bay. To that meeting on Friday, 15th July, 1749, came Paul Mascerene, the retiring lieutenant-governor, five of his councillors, and deputies from the Acadian villages. The records of what then transpired show the temper of the new administration. Proceedings opened with Cornwallis reading His Majesty's Commission and Instructions. The new Governor was to issue a proclamation to the Acadians reminding them of their position as subjects of his Britannic Majesty. They were to take regular oaths of allegiance, without any reserve whatsoever. They were to be allowed their priests but provisions were to be made to encourage conversion to Protestantism. Every channel of possible communication between old and new settlers within the province was to be explored, in the hope that the influence of the new Protestant immigrants would encourage the Acadians to display a greater loyalty to the British.

The records go on to say that Mascerene rose at this point and gave the form of the oath that the Acadians had taken in the past:

> Je . . . promets and Jure sincerement en Foi de Chrétien que Je serai entièrement fidèle and obeirai vraiment Sa Majesté Le Roi George le Second que je reconnais pour le Souverain Seigneur de l'Acadie ou nouvelle Ecosse.
> Ainsi Dieu me soit en Aide.

The Council Minutes continue:

> Col. Mascerene informed the Council that the French pretended that when they took this Oath it was upon Condition, that it should be understood that they always be exempted from bearing Arms, therefore it was moved to add to the Oath this clause, & Ce Serment Je prens sans réserve.

But the Council was of opinion that no Conditions appear in the Oath they have hitherto taken and subscribed, which Oath is as strong as any Oath of Allegiance can be, it would only be necessary to let the French know that they must take the oath without any Conditional Clauses understood or any reservation whatsoever.[3]

The picture of the Council's agreeing that all that was needed was to inform the Acadians of what they should do, in order to have it done, betrays an English misjudgement of the situation in Nova Scotia as grave as that of the Acadians' misjudgement in trusting in their policy of neutrality.

The Acadians had insisted on neutrality since 1713. Mascerne considered that during the recent hostilities Acadian neutrality had enabled the English to retain Nova Scotia, writing that the "French Inhabitants keep still in their fidelity" and were not "in any ways joyn'd with the Enemy." He did not consider that any more active support of the English could reasonably be expected of them. Cornwallis now informed the Acadians that they would take the "Oath of Allegiance to his Majesty in the same manner as all English Subjects do", thereby asserting implicity that he expected more from them than had his predecessors. The meeting ended with the Acadians being given a copy of the Declaration which Cornwallis had prepared to be issued to them. This opened with the announcement that a number of British subjects were to be settled in Nova Scotia for the improvement and extension of its trade and fisheries. The Acadians, it continued, had in the past been dealt with most indulgently, having been allowed "the entirely free exercise of their Religion and the quiet and peaceable Possession of their Lands", but that this treatment had not been met with an appropriate loyalty. In future the Acadians could only expect similar leniency "Provided that the said Inhabitants do within Three months from the date of the Declaration take the Oaths of Allegiance."[4] They were asked to report back from their settlements within two weeks and to ensure that deputies from other villages came to see Cornwallis as soon as possible.

Superficially the English policy appeared to be based upon an overly optimistic estimation of the possibilities of Acadian co-operation. Its real foundation, however, was that Cornwallis had been given much greater resources for the government of Nova Scotia than had his predecessors. He had arrived with instructions for the establishment of a new English stronghold at Halifax, with over twenty-five hundred new colonists, and with soldiers who had, until recently, garrisoned Louisbourg and would now act as veteran troops for the control of Nova Scotia. By 1751, Halifax was a settlement of more than six hundred houses within a palisade, and Protestant immigrants had established themselves sufficiently at Lunenberg for the Acadian monopoly of European settlement within the colony to be broken. However unwilling the Acadians would be to recognise the fact, the English were now committed to making Nova Scotia an effective part of their empire in North America.

At the same time, of equal importance to the Acadians, there was an equally strong desire on the part of the French to make the peninsula once more theirs. It is worth remarking that the peace treaty of 1748 had provided for an international commission to settle exactly the boundaries of the territories ceded in 1713 under the name of "Acadie or Nova Scotia", and that within the conference room the French claimed that only the peninsula itself had been ceded, while the English claimed the territory spread from the banks of the St. Lawrence to the limits of Massachusetts. The governor of Quebec, La Galissonière, commenting to the government of France on the British position, wrote:

> Si nous abandonnions à l'Angleterre ce terrain qui comprend plus de 180 lieue de côtes, c'est-à-dire presque autant qu'il y en a de Bayonne à Dunkerque, il faudrait renoncer à toute communciation par terre du Canada avec l'Acadie et l'île Royale et à toute moyen de secourir l'un et de reprendre l'autre."[5]

For neither the French nor the English was Aix-la-Chapelle more than a signal for the rebuilding of their respective strengths in North America; and for both, Nova Scotia appeared to be of paramount strategic importance. While the English built Halifax and established new groups of immigrants within the peninsula, the French increased the number of their troops at the mouth of the St. John River and occupied the Chignecto

Isthmus. At the same time they used every possible influence to retain the attachment of the Indians to the French cause. This was made easier for them by the return to North America of the Abbé Le Loutre. He had been a missionary to the MicMacs since 1738 and his influence over them was very great. In the summer of 1749 Bigot, the new intendant of New France, visited Louisbourg where he received news of a possible alliance between the English and the Indians. He reported to his superiors that he and Le Loutre had decided such possibility must be defeated at all costs, and he gave Le Loutre the necessary arms, money and presents to achieve this end. As a result, in September 1749 Cornwallis received a declaration of war from this tribe and their allies the Abenakis.

Thus the early months of the regime of Cornwallis saw the Indians an obvious menace, the French ever watchful for an opportunity to improve their position, and the Acadians temporising once more over the oath. They acted on the assumption that this governor was no different from the rest; they were convinced of the rectitude of their own past conduct and of their right to parlay. The Acadian answer to the demand from Cornwallis for an unqualified oath was that they were willing to take "notre ancien serment avec exemption d'armes à nos et à nos hoirs [sic]"[6] but should this be refused, they would leave their lands. Cornwallis realised clearly what the Acadians needed. He wrote to his superiors in London, "I think 'tis necessary to show them that 'tis in our power to master them or to protect them,"[7] and enclosed detailed plans to this end. He was never able to achieve his aims, however; and while English power was being unostentatiously strengthened in Nova Scotia, French power was wielded not only on the borders but within the colony itself, both the power of the regular army and the power of the Indians acting in the interest of the French. The situation was much more violent than it had been in the years immediately after Utrecht: then the menace of the Indians had been theoretical, now the winter of 1749-50 saw them within the Acadian villages, capturing a company of English engineers at Grand-Pré. After 1713 the French had merely expressed their wish for Acadie; now French forts were built on the edge of Acadian lands, in particular in the neighbourhood of Beauséjour. Also, at the time of Utrecht the French had made representations to the Acadians to persuade them to move to French-held lands; in the spring of 1750 the Indians, led by the Abbé Le Loutre, burnt Beaubassin to the ground in order to persuade its inhabitants to cross on to the mainland. In sum, at the time of the treaty of Utrecht the fate of Nova Scotia was the subject of debate; after the treaty of Aix-la-Chapelle it was a matter of guns. The Acadian reaction towards the debate had been a policy of neutrality; towards the fighting, they made a considerable attempt to follow the same policy.

Acadian accounts of their actions between 1748 and 1755 were written after the deportation. One can compare the versions given by Acadians to authorities in several of the North American colonies, such as Massachusetts, Pennsylvania and Virginia, with those given to authorities in France. Contemporary accounts of Acadian action during these same years come from their administrators, their neighbours, both those of New England and of Louisbourg, and from various French officials. The picture which emerges from these records is that of people becoming more and more enmeshed in a war fought across their lands by other powers. Their own actions betrayed only one consistency: an attempt to avoid reprisals by both sides. Their major difficulty was that English power within the colony was to prove the more durable, but French power was the more obviously threatening during the early years of the 1750s. In a letter describing the situation in Nova Scotia in 1750, for his superiors in London, Cornwallis wrote that the French had gathered together on the borders of the colony a force of twenty-five hundred men, made up of Canadians, Indians and some Acadians. He judged that the Acadians had been brought in by means of force and noted that many on this border were no longer attending to their lands. "They make no scruple to declare this proceeding is entirely against their inclination but that La Corne (the French commander) and Loutre threaten them with a general massacre by savages if they remain in the Province."[8] There is no question that during these years the French were using every means in their power to force the Acadians either to rise against the English, or to move to French territory. Nor is there any doubt about the influence of Le Loutre. A French officer wrote to his superiors in the autumn of 1750 that

Il est sûr que sans ce missionaire qui a fait croire aux acadiens ce qu'il a voulu et leur a promois beaucoup, ils seroient tres tranquiles et que les Anglois seroient de même à Chibouctou et trés amis des sauvages.[9]

In sum, the development of English strength was slow and the menace of French arms constant during the first year of the administration of Cornwallis. As a result, in the summer of 1750 the Acadians were no more ready than they had ever been to swear an unqualified oath of allegiance to the English. The English were equally unprepared to see the Acadians leave Nova Scotia *en masse* or to admit Acadian neutrality.

The second year of Cornwallis's administration saw a repetition of the situation. English strength within the peninsula imperceptibly increased. Major Lawrence, who would later be the lieutenant-general of Nova Scotia when the deportation took place, prevented further infiltration of French troops into the colony by holding the fort named after him on the isthmus. At the same time, the French were successful in persuading, by blandishments and threats, some two hundred families to leave for Ile St. Jean, the St. John River valley, or the vicinity of Beauséjour itself.* These migrants soon found that their new conditions had very little to recommend them. Many came back to English territory within two years. They found themselves cultivating new land and facing a French administration which expected even more from them than had that of Halifax. In May 1751, for example, the commander at Louisbourg issued an ordnance to the Acadians within his command, stating that they must swear an oath of loyalty and be incorporated into the militia, or be declared rebels to the King of France and expelled from their new lands. This same ordnance spoke of some of the Acadians being guilty of the worst sort of ingratitude, rendering themselves thereby unworthy of participating in the grace of the King of France, because they would not join in the fighting.[10]

---

*The number of Acadians involved in such activities during the 1750s is a most contentious matter, estimations depending upon estimations of the total Acadian population. This has been put as high as 18,000 in 1755 by some writers. The figure used here will be substantiated in the next chapter.

There is no denying that by 1751 Cornwallis had made the English presence in Nova Scotia much stronger than it had ever been but, at the same time, there had been strengthening of French forces on the limits of the peninsula. Under the command of Major Lawrence a force of three hundred English soldiers tried and failed to capture Beauséjour that summer. In the light of his wish to show the force of the English, Cornwallis might have been content to have that many troops at his disposal, but their failure could hardly reinforce Acadian belief in the ultimate victory of English arms. At the same time while the new German immigrants were being settled within the colony, on the whole satisfactorily, it was also true that some of them deserted to the French forces, and could hardly be described as an immediate access of strength to the English. As the final winter of his administration began, 1751-52, Cornwallis expressed moderate satisfaction over the state of the colony. He felt that London should accord it even more men and money, and that at least half of its troubles came from the willingness of New York and Rhode Island to trade with Louisbourg. As to the Acadians, he considered that there was every chance of their being made into reasonable citizens, if only they could be removed from the influence of their priests.

The question of the Acadians' religion, and of their supply of priests, had always been a major concern of their English administrators. Eighteenth-century England permitted a much greater amount of religious freedom than did either contemporary France or other societies in North America. While Catholics in eighteenth-century England were barred from the exercise of direct political power, they were to be found at all levels of society and their disabilities very rarely mounted to the level of a persecution. English administrators would thus be accustomed to the legal existence of Catholicism. In France, however, Huguenots suffered from the Revocation of the Edict of Nantes, and the rigidity of New England Protestantism needs no emphasis. What made the Acadians' position of a particular thorny character for the English was that their priests were supplied by France and were linked to the jurisdiction of the Bishop of Quebec. Given the strategic situation of Nova Scotia and the general belief in the unbreakable alliance between religion and politics in French life, it is not surprising that the English looked upon the priests sent to the Acadians as probable spies and *agents provocateurs* for the French cause. This judgement was, of course, justified by men like Le Loutre and quietly contradicted by the existence of other priests, such as Daudin, who spent their energies completely within the permitted bounds of ecclesiastical action.

As far as assigning responsibility for the deportation of 1755 is concerned, the influence of the priests upon the Acadians is only one factor among many. In attempting to discover the limits of this influence, however, a study of the ecclesiastical records shows not only much individuality among the priests themselves but considerable divergence among the hierarchy as to what the main concerns of a priest working with the Acadians should be. The Bishop of Quebec has left several letters, written during the 1740s and 1750s, in which he insisted that the priests must conduct themselves with circumspection and indulge in no political activity which would give the English grounds for their expulsion: the cure of souls was to be their only aim.[11] On the other hand, the Vicar-General of the church in New France, the Abbé de l'Isle Dieu, who resided in France and was largely responsible for the recruitment of the priests for the Acadians, considered that the salvation of their souls could be found only on French territory. He fully backed the efforts of Le Loutre and endeavoured to send priests directly to him, so that their opinions would not be influenced by anyone else.[12] It is not surprising that this subject has been yet one more matter for debate among historians.

At the time of Cornwallis's judgement there were three priests actually working among the Acadian population of Nova Scotia and, of course, Le Loutre, working with the Indians on the border of the colony. Their presence would certainly remind the Acadians of the French, but the Acadians would not necessarily respond to this with an unquestioning loyalty to the fleur-de-lis. Acadian actions before Aix-la-Chapelle, in the judgement not only of Mascerene but also of the French officers sent among them to procure their aid, was a demonstration above all of loyalty to themselves. In the eyes of their contemporaries, however, and in the eyes of many later historians, such a loyalty was inadmissable since it involved a refusal to "take sides" in a question where emotional factors demanded the expression of a preference. On the one hand, it was apparently obvious that French-speaking Catholics would feel the need to support the policies of France. On the other hand it was apparently obvious that a sense of civic responsibility would make the Acadians give a dutiful obedience to the power that had allowed their peaceful development over forty years. But the Acadians were too conscious of the fluctuations of political fortune. Inhabitants of lands which had changed hands fourteen times within a century, with a well-founded knowledge of English power within Nova Scotia and of French power surrounding Nova Scotia, the Acadians gave emotional loyalty to their families, their villages, their lands. Loyalty to either France or England, for the majority of the Acadians, would depend almost exclusively on the ability of these powers to enforce their control of Acadian villages.

The possibilities of a peaceful relationship between Acadian and English, even in the 1750s, can be seen from the short governorship of Peregrine Hopson. Cornwallis left Nova Scotia in the spring of 1752 and by the summer the new governor was in power. He held office for little more than a year. He was on good terms with his counterpart at Louisbourg and from the outset was optimistic about the situation in the colony. In his first report to the Lords of Trade, Hopson reported that the French Inhabitants had no intention of leaving the colony and he had no wish for them to go.[13] By January 1753, Hopson was convinced that peace had come to the borders of his colony and considered that his major problem was the possibility of corruption among the Justices of the Inferior Courts. Even spring did not bring the usual immediate revival of trouble, partly because Le Loutre was in Europe. At the end of the summer  of 1753, Hopson summed up the position of the colony for his superiors in London. His verdict was much the same as the judgement of Cornwallis on the situation in 1749: the French were strong on the borders of the colony, the governors of Quebec and Louisbourg openly aided border raids, Nova Scotia needed more aid, and the Acadians were prevented from showing "a firm attachment"[14] to the British by their fear of Indian and French reprisals.

The Acadians had every reason to be of the same opinion as Hopson and to consider that no radical alteration had taken

place in their situation during the four years following 1749. After complaining about their attitude in the matter, the English had let the question of an unqualified oath drop. The French were still on the borders of the peninsula and their installations in the immediate region were, if anything, strengthened. The existence of Halifax and the German Protestants at Lunenberg did not seem to have altered the military situation in favour of the English. Nevertheless, to the Acadians, life in French territory was by no means more appealing than life under English rule on the lands of their ancestors. The English demands were no more unreasonable than those made by the French to the Acadians who had moved to their territory. In fact, since the Acadians had a long tradition of co-operating with the English only in those areas in which the Acadians wished to co-operate, life under English government could be preferred to that under the French. In sum, with the arrival of Major Charles Lawrence as the lieutenant-governor of the colony in 1753, the Acadians had no reason to suspect a radical alteration of their lives.

Yet this is precisely what happened, and one of the reasons is the convictions of Lawrence himself. Mascerene, Hopson, and most of their predecessors had governed Nova Scotia with the belief that the Acadians were a fixed part of its population, that ideas of their exile were impractical, and that their attitude towards an unqualified oath of allegiance was an annoyance rather than a source of serious perturbation. Lawrence, however, saw the matter in a very different light. This was partly the result of his experiences. He was above all a military man, born and brought up in a cantonment, a major at the age of thirty-seven. He had first come to Louisbourg in 1747 and since then had been employed mainly on duties concerned with the security of the colony. He had a first-hand knowledge of the strength of the French on the borders of the colony and of the weakness of the English elsewhere. Lawrence summed up his position in a letter written to his superiors some nine months after his appointment. After commenting on the unco-operative attitude of the Acadians, he went on to say:

> While they remain without taking oaths to His Majesty (which they will never do till they are forced) and have incendiary French priests among them, there are no hopes

of their amendment. As they possess the best and largest tracts of land in this province, it cannot be settled with any effect while they remain in this situation. And tho' I would be very far from attempting such a step without your Lordships' approbation, yet I cannot help being of the opinion that it would be much better, if they refuse the oaths, that they were away. The only ill consequences that can attend their going would be their taking arms and joining the Indians to distress our settlements, as they are numerous and our troops much divided; tho' I believe that a very large part of the inhabitants would submit to any terms rather than take up arms on either side; but that is only my conjecture and not to be depended on in so critical a circumstance.[15]

In other words, Lawrence could envisage clearly the functioning of Nova Scotia without the presence of the Acadians. He thought of the strategic questions of the colony as being of fundamental importance, and considered all other matters to be subordinate to this factor.

The historical controversy over the events of 1755 has resulted in literally hundreds of books and pamphlets, of which two hundred had been published by the end of the nineteenth century. Part of the interest stems from the sheer complications of the matter; it is that of detection: what exactly happened? to whom? by whom? for what motive? Even more interest, however, has been caused by the apparently obvious ideological explanations of the matter. The deportation of the Acadians has been considered as a prime example of national and religious rivalries, because the labels of Catholicism, Protestantism, French and English can be attached to opposing sections of the groups of people involved. Many of the works which have appeared about the Acadian deportation are informed with a driving demand to assign guilt and innocence in the matter. Yet the reality is much more complex and much more human than such explanations would suggest. What happened in 1755 was the result as much of immediate individual choices and of personal action as it was of past traditions and of the concatenation of official government policies and international pressures.

As the summer of 1754 drew to a close, the external factors which would affect events in Nova Scotia began to take shape.

Soon "Washington's first shot beyond the Alleghenies" would completely shatter the hollow pretence of peace in North America. The Governor of Massachusetts, still that Shirley who had fought so hard for the retention of Louisbourg, entered into an assidous correspondence with Lawrence, whose immediate superior he was, on the security problems of their two colonies. As the winter went on, the two men laid plans to clear the French from the north shore of the Bay of Fundy and from the isthmus of Chignecto. At the same time, with the end of 1754, England and France condemned each other for reopening hostilities, and each set about readying an army for America. By early 1755, England had ordered her fleet to attack any French vessels sailing for that continent and as a rejoinder, France had fitted out eighteen ships to carry some three thousand men overseas, for the support of her colonies in the New World. Once more open warfare for the control of a continent was begun, and this time its most immediate effect would be the social tragedy of the Acadians.

Chapter IV

Decision and Consequence: 1755

By the early summer of 1755, the plans which Lawrence and Shirley had drawn up the previous winter had been successfully carried into effect. Together they had commissioned Colonel Monckton to deal with the French forts on the borders of Nova Scotia. With mainly New England troops at his command, the latter had captured Beauséjour at the end of the second week of June and the rest of the French garrisons, Fort Gaspereau on the Atlantic side and the French strongholds on the St. John River, fell soon after. By the end of the month, the northern territory of Nova Scotia was, for the first time, securely in English hands. The Indians were sufficiently impressed by this series of victories to end their attacks on the English. With such victories to strengthen him, Lawrence now turned to the problem of the Acadians.

In June 1755, the majority of these people were proving Lawrence's estimation of them to have been correct. He had suggested, in the letter quoted in the previous chapter, that he privately believed that the greater part of the Acadians would do anything rather than take up arms. Most of them were fully occupied with their habitual tasks on their lands. Many of those in the Minas area gave a fundamental proof of their neutrality by surrendering their guns in the spring, when they were commanded so to do, an act of tremendous consequence in the circumstances of eighteenth-century Nova Scotia.[1] Others, of course, had co-operated with the French. When Beauséjour fell, some two hundred Acadians were discovered among the men defending the fort. It was difficult even for Monckton to decide whether the majority of these were there of their own free will or whether, as they all claimed, they had been pressed into service under pain of death. As June came to an end, Lawrence met in Halifax with the elected delegates from all the Acadian villages, and while the Acadians offered to renew the oath of neutrality Lawrence once more attempted to extract an unqualified oath of allegiance from them.

The constitutional structure of Nova Scotia at this juncture was founded on the statutes governing the colony of Virginia, instructions to this effect having been sent to Annapolis Royal in 1719, and there was no question of an elected assembly.[2] Great power resided in a selected Council and ultimate authority, subject only to revision from London, was in the hands of the governor or lieutenant-governor who was actually administering Nova Scotia at the time. The political maneuverings which led to the deportation can be traced clearly through the records of this Council, which met on its own and also with the Acadian delegates. From these same records one matter is quite clear: the Acadians were convinced of their right to discuss and debate, and the Councillors were equally convinced of the Acadian right only to hear and accept. The first confrontation took place on 3rd July, 1755.[3] The Acadians from Minas immediately showed that recent events in the colony had in nowise altered their traditional policy. Once more they offered an oath of loyalty on condition that their neutrality was respected. Once more they were told that "His Majesty had disapproved of the manner of their taking the oath before," and they were dismissed from the Council Chamber but not sent back to the villages. They were confined in Halifax. Once the Acadians had gone, the permanent members of the Council laid down their policy for the future; the oath was to be offered to the Acadians; if refused, it was not to be offered again; those who refused were to be deported.

In examining the English policy, it would be helpful if one could discover a note from Lawrence as to his intentions at this point. Without putting ideas into his head, it is hard to decide whether he believed that the Acadians would refuse the oath *en masse,* or whether he considered that they would be aware of his position of strength and quickly capitulate. After the event, documents rationalising the policy abound, and historians have frequently traced actions performed in 1755 back to vague comments expressed by long-dead officials thirty years before. At any rate, within the colony the immediate, visible consequences of this meeting of the first week of July was general perturbation and rumour. The tension was heightened for the English by the arrival in Halifax on 9th July of Admiral Boscawen, fresh from his fight with the French fleet off Newfoundland. He had captured the *Lys* and the *Alcide* but the rest had escaped him.

On July 15th, Boscawen and his second-in-command, Mostyn, who had arrived in Halifax on July 11th, joined the deliberations of the Council. At this meeting it was decided that the two thousand New England volunteers, still present in Nova Scotia after their action along the Bay of Fundy in the spring, should be retained a little longer. The decision to deport the Acadians should they refuse an unqualified oath was reaffirmed. As far as Lawrence was concerned this reaffirmation was an important political support, because Boscawen was the highest-ranking military authority in the area. In his despatch to the Board of Trade, written three days later on July 18th, he informed the Board of Trade that he was ordering the Acadians to elect new deputies to confer with him and that if they refused to take the oath, he intended "to rid the Province of such perfidious subjects."[4] On July 23rd the news reached Halifax that Braddock's army had been defeated and General Braddock himself killed. On the 25th July, the first of the new delegates from the Acadian villages reached Halifax.

They were from Annapolis Royal and carried a memorandum to place before the Council. In it they protested that they had always been loyal to George II and were willing to surrender the rest of their firearms in proof of this. They were willing to abide by the oath they had sworn earlier but they would take no new one. After having met with the Council they produced the following document:

> Inasmuch as as a report is in circulation among us, the French inhabitants of this province, that His Excellency the Governor demands of us an oath of obedience conformable in some manner, to that of the natural subjects of His Majesty King George the Second, and as, in consequence we are morally certain that several of our inhabitants are detained and put to inconvenience at Halifax for that object; if the above are his intentions with respect to us, we all take the liberty of representing to His Excellency, and to all the inhabitants, that we and our fathers, having

taken an oath of fidelity, which has been approved of several times in the name of the King, and under the privileges of which we have lived faithful, and obedient, and protected by His Majesty the King of Great Britain, according to the letters and proclamations of His Excellency Governor Shirley, dated 16th of September 1746, and that of the 21st of October, 1747, we will never prove so fickle as to take an oath which changes, ever so little, the conditions and the privileges obtained for us by our soverign and our fathers in the past.

And as we are well aware that the King, our master, loves and protects only constant, faithful, and free subjects, and as it is by virtue of his kindness, and of the fidelity which we have always preserved towards His Majesty, that he has granted to us, and that he still continues to grant to us, the entire possession of our property and the free and public exercise of the Roman Catholic Religion, we desire to continue to be faithful and dutiful in the same manner we were allowed to be by His Excellency Mr. Richard Philipps.

Charity for our detained inhabitants and their innocence, oblige us to beg Your Excellency, to allow yourself to be touched by their miseries, and to restore to them that liberty which we ask for them, with all possible submission and the most profound respect.[5]

As other delegations from elsewhere in the colony arrived, they all produced the same type of memorial, attesting to past loyalty, present good intent, and complete obduracy on the point of a new and unqualified oath.

Whatever one may take as the credibility of this document, it shows the Acadians as having, firstly, an historical conception of their position within Nova Scotia, one determined by past negotiations and precedents. Secondly, it reveals a belief in Acadian rights, granted by the King of England but nevertheless rights to hold land and to the public exercise of Catholicism. Thirdly, it shows an awareness of themselves as distinct from "the natural subjects" of King George, an awareness the Acadians would carry into exile and which would lead to one of their number stating to a French official in St. Mâlo, in 1773, that they would consider what the latter had suggested to the chiefs of their "nation". This affirmation of nationality was the keynote of the Acadians both immediately before and during their exile, and it was an affirmation that went for the most part royally unheard.

The final confrontation of Acadian delegates and Nova Scotion Council took place on Monday, July 28th, at ten o'clock in the morning. Six members of the Council were present: Lawrence; Benjamin Green, a New England trader now resident in Halifax; John Collier, an English officer turned settler; John Rous, a Boston sailor, now a captain in the Royal Navy; Jonathan Belcher, a son of a former governor of Massachusetts, recently named chief justice in Nova Scotia; William Cotterell, Secretary of the Province. There were also present two representatives of the Fleet, Boscawen and Mostyn. The Acadians produced once more their arguments in favour of their position, including the most undeniable, but in the eyes of the Council, most arrogant one of all: that no amount of oath-taking would keep them loyal should they wish to rebel, the best proof of their behaviour being the neutrality of the past action. Their arguments were unheeded. The Council had decided that the oath had been offered a sufficiency of times. Belcher produced a document as to the legality of deporting the Acadians, and the Council as a whole informed the delegates that the decision had been made.

The deportation was immediately set in train. On the 31st July, 1755, Lawrence wrote a long letter to Monckton. He said:

. . . it is accordingly determined that they (the French Inhabitants of the Province) shall be removed out of the Country as soon as possible . . . orders are given for a sufficient number of transports to be sent up . . . by whom you will receive particular instructions as to the manner of their being disposed of, the place of their destination, and every other thing necessary for that purpose.

In the meantime, it will be necessary to keep this measure as secret as possible, as well to prevent their attempting to escape, as to carry off their cattle etc., and the better to effect this you will endeavour to fall upon some strategem to get the men both young and old (especially the heads of families) into your power and detain them until transports shall arrive so as that they may be ready to be shipped off. . . . As their whole stock of Cattle and Corn is

forfeited to the Crown by their rebellion, and must be secured and applyd towards a remibursement of the expense the government will be at in transporting them out of the Country, care must be had that nobody make any bargain for purchasing them under any colour or pretense whatever; if they do the sale will be void, for the inhabitants have now (since the Order in Council) no property in them, nor will they be allowed to carry away the least thing but their ready money and household furniture.
The officers commanding the Fort at Piziquid and the Garrison of Annapolis Royal have nearly the same orders in relation to the interior Inhabitants. . . .
It is agreed that the inhabitants shall have on board with them, one pound of Flouw [sic] and half a pound of bread pr Day for each person, and a pound of beef pr week to each, the Bread and the Beef will be sent to you by Transports from Halifax, the Flour you have already in store.[6]

The diverse interpretations of this letter by historians provide an excellent example of the division of opinion on the deportation. For Lauvrière, what one needed to retain from this letter and from the supplementary instructions sent to Monckton on August 8th was:

". . . la précision minutieuse des instruction depuis longtemps élaborées, la lâche traitrise des procedes d'arrestation récommandés, la cruelle parsimonie des rations préscrites et l'-étrange sollicitude montrée, ici comme aillieurs, a l'égard, non pas des gens, mais du bétail".[7] For Brebner, however, the documents carried a totally different message. He wrote that "Lawrence had attempted in the beginning to be very painstaking in preparation, and by contemporary standards, careful to provide adequate ship-room for his victims, allotting two persons to a shipping ton, and allowing methodically for their provisioning from captured food-stuffs with necessary supplement from Halifax."[8]

The deportation of the Acadians was attended with death and destruction, although the major loss of life came when the ships had left. Nothing happened during 1755, nor during the succeeding years, which saw a continuing attempt to eradicate the Acadians from Nova Scotia, to approach the statistics of death and misery compiled during the actual transport and exile. For example, the *Cornwallis* had left Chignecto for South Carolina with 417 Acadians on board. When she docked at Charleston only 210 were still alive.[9] Lawrence, as Brebner has written, did indeed lose his temper, but this was nothing unusual and its impact on the way in which the deportation was carried out is debatable. On August 11th, Lawrence wrote again to Monckton that "the Inhabitants . . . are allowed to carry with them their household furniture; yet they must not put on board quantities of useless Rubbish to encumber the Vessels."[10] In instructions of the same date, which were sent not specifically to Monckton but to those dealing with the Chignecto settlements generally, Lawrence demanded that the Acadians be obliged to come in "by burning the Villages and destroying everything that can afford them the least Shelter." In September, Monckton was informed by Lawrence that "I would have you not' wait for the Wives and Children coming in but Ship Off the Men without them".[11] He was still repeating this order at the end of the month, and at the end of October was once more counselling the burning of villages in order that there would be no shelter available to those who escaped. However, the way in which the Acadians were treated depended less on the advice of Lawrence than upon the characters of the officers in charge. Nothing would be done by the latter in contradiction of the main purpose, deportation, but a considerable amelioration of methods was achieved by those officers who wished so to do.

Many of those involved evidently disliked their work. An old man contacted by Dr. Brown, a Scottish doctor much interested in compiling the history of the Acadians, wrote:

In 1755 I was a very humble Instrument in sending Eighteen hundred of these suffering mortels out of the Province, in 1763 as Commissionary General to the army serving in North America, it became my duty . . . to embark Thirty-Five Thousand Loyalists at New York . . . and I trust all in my power was done to soften the Affliction of the Acadians and Alleviate the sufferings of the Loyalists.[12]

Major John Handfield, whose work was centered around Annapolis Royal, wrote to Winslow, who was the other senior officer besides Monckton involved in the business, as follows: "I heartily join with you in wishing that we were both of us got over this most disagreeable and troublesome part of the Service."[13] Winslow himself has left a journal[14] of the fateful summer and autumn. This together with his letters, and those of others, brings out clearly the attitude of the officers of the army. One such letter from Winslow, that of September 5th to Captain Murray, who was engaged in clearing the area around Fort Edward, says: "Things are Now Very Heavy on my Harte and hands, wish we had more men, but as it is Shall, I question not, be able to Skuffel Throh."[15] On the whole, the soldiery in attempting the task before them, felt the deportation of recalcitrant subjects, excessive and a planned campaign of terror was not added to the misery of the circumstances.

But for the Acadians the tragedy was the destruction of their society, the dispersal of their close-knit families, the breaking of their related communities. In the same way that some interpretations of 1755 have frequently stressed national and religious ideologies as the sole cause of the debacle, others have suggested that, since property was lost, greed was the motive. But property was burnt rather than looted, villages destroyed rather than re-inhabited, money lost to the government through the necessity of paying for soldiers and ships rather than gained by confiscations, and the land, at least temporarily, lost to the wilderness again, rather than being promptly re-settled. The essence of the events of the summer and autumn of 1755 was that it saw the first real conquest of the Acadians. Their reactions were diverse. Some were so stunned that Winslow wrote to Lawrence, while he was still waiting for transport to reach him at Grand-Pré, that he did not think the Acadians were yet fully persuaded that they were "actually to be removed."[16] Others fought back bitterly, though on the whole ineffectively. Evidence from letters of the Abbé Le Guerne, who remained in what is now south New Brunswick until August 1757, gives vivid pictures of women and children taking to the woods to escape deportation, of people fleeing with nothing to escape the soldiery, their settlements in flames behind them.[17]

Then there are success stories of more organised resistance.

The report of the first prison-camp tunnel, is that of some eighty-six Acadians who got away from Fort Lawrence "by making a Hole under Ground from the Barrack through the South Curtain above Thirty feet. It is worse as they are all people whose wives were not come in, and of Chipoudi Pitcoudiack and Memramcook".[18] Even on board ship hope was not lost: one group captured their captors and sailed the ship back to the Bay of Fundy, there managing to land and flee northward to the upper reaches of the St. John River.[19] But these were exceptions to the general rule. The vast majority of the Acadian population of Nova Scotia was deported in 1755.

The statistics of the operation are extremely difficult to compute. Firstly, estimations of the Acadian population of 1755 differ widely and secondly, the deportation, although it took place primarily in 1755, actually lasted longer. The proscription against the Acadians in Nova Scotia lasted nine years. One year after the Peace of Paris they were once more granted the right to settle and own land in Nova Scotia. As late as 1762, however, Acadians were still being sent from the colony. Some historians consider that as many as ten thousand people were displaced during this period and others put the figure around six thousand. In my own estimation the Acadian population numbered some ten thousand in 1755, of which six thousand were deported that same year. Of the remainder I think approximately two thousand were rounded up and exiled during the succeeding years. The fate of the rest was either voluntary migration, death, or a harried and persecuted existence within Nova Scotia until the change in their political condition was wrought in 1764. There is one shred of certainty in this statistical maze: the number of those who came forward in 1764 to take an oath of allegiance to George III was computed at less than one thousand, forming some hundred and sixty-five families.[20] The attorney-general of the colony, Jonathan Belcher, a member of the Council which made the decision to deport, estimated in a report he made to the home authorities on the matter that the number of Acadians in Nova Scotia in 1755 was eight thousand.[21]

The question of reporting the action to the home government raises the question of the responsibility in the matter of the Imperial authorities. This question was a subject for much debate at the end of the nineteenth century and beginning of the twentieth. Accustomed to the Imperial structures of their own era, men such as Casgrain and Richard did not take fully into account the conditions of eighteenth-century life. The Lords of Trade, and other official bodies concerned with Nova Scotia and the Acadians, were credited with spending much greater time and energy on the matter than they actually did, and with pursuing with vigor a more coherent policy towards questions raised by colony and inhabitants than was actually the case. There was little appreciation that eighteenth-century politics and technology together gave the colonial administrator the widest possible liberty of action. For the men in power in London, whether permanent members of the bureaucracy or transient administrators, the imperative was success. A letter sent to Lawrence from Their Lordships, dated the 13th August, 1755, which, of course, did not reach him until well after the Acadians had been uprooted, is a fair summary of official English opinion on the Nova Scotia situation at that time:

> Sir,
> Whatever Construction may be put by the French upon the word "Pardonne" in the Fourth Article of the Capitulation granted to the Commander and Governor of Beauséjour, It is observed, by your letter of ye 28th June, that you had given Orders to Colonel Monckton, *to drive the deserted French inhabitants, at all Events out of the* Country, It does not, clearly, appear, whether you mean, to drive away, all the French inhabitants of the Peninsula, which amount to many Thousands, or, such of them, as you say, in your State of the English and French Forts, transmitted here in Governor Shirley's letter of the 8th of December last, were settled, to the number of about 8,000 [sic] Families, in five, or six Villages in the Neighbourhood of Beauséjour, when evacuated by the garrison; the latter seems, rather, to have been your intention, as you add *That if Mr. Monckton wants the Assistance of the French deserted Inhabitants in putting the Troops under Cover as the barracks in the French Fort were demolished, he may at first make them do all the Service in their Power.* Let your Intention have been what it will, It is not doubted, but that you will have acted upon a Strict Principle of immediate and indespensible Security to your Government,

and not without having considered the pernicious consequences that may arise from any Alarm which may have
been given to the whole Body of French Neutrals, and
how suddenly an Insurrection may follow from Despair;
or what an additional Number of useful Subjects may be
given by their Flight to the French king; It cannot, therefore, be too much recommended to you, to use the greatest caution and Prudence in your Conduct, towards these
neutrals, and to assure such of Them, as may be trusted,
especially upon their taking the Oaths to His Majesty, and
His Government, That They may remain in the quiet Possession of their Settlements, under proper Regulations:
What has led to a more particular Notice of this Part of
your Letter, is the following Proposal, That was made no
longer ago than in the Month of May last, by the French
Ambassador, vizt. [sic] "That all the French Inhabitants
of the Peninsula should have three years allowed them to
remove from Thence, with their Effects, and should be
favoured with all means of facilitating this Removal, which
the English would, it is said. undoubtedly look upon as
very advantageous to Themselves." Whereupon His Majesty was pleased to order an Answer to be given and which
I now send you, for your particular Information, in the
following words. vitz: [sic], "In regard to the Three
Years Transmigration, proposed for the French Inhabitants
of the Peninsula, it would be depriving Great Britain of a
very considerable Number of useful Subjects, if such
Transmigration should extend to the French, who were
Inhabitants there, at the time of the Treaty of Utrecht, and
to their descendants.
                              T. Robinson.[22]
                              I am, etc.,

In sum, the policy of London was less concerned with the
details of administration than with the final result. This is
shown even more clearly by the immediate response made by
the Lords of Trade to the despatch in which Lawrence informed
them of the real scope of his operations. This was to make
him governor. Their comment on the expulsion itself did not
appear until spring 1756 and reads:

. . . we have laid that part of your letter which relates to
the Removal of the French Inhabitants and the Steps you

took in the Execution of this Measure before His Majesty's Secretary of State and as you represent it to have been indispensably necessary for the Security and Protection of the Province in the Present critical Situation of Our Affairs We doubt not but that your Conduct herein will meet with His Majesty's approbation.[23]

The Canadian archivist Placide Gaudet, himself of Acadian descent, concluded that the Imperial authorities would have held out against the deportation of the Acadians if informed before the event, if only from fear of the consequences of failure, but accepted it complaisantly as a *fait accompli* which had strengthened the British position in North America at a time when support was badly needed. This seems to me a fair conclusion to the question.

For the Acadians themselves the question of the final responsibility for their eviction was overshadowed in 1755 by the events of the eviction itself. Their immediate destination was one of the other English colonies in North America. The captains of the ships on which they sailed carried a letter to the respective governors of the colonies to which they were destined. Signed by Lawrence, dated Halifax, August 11th, 1755, it informed its recipient that "the success that has attended His Majesty's Arms . . . Furnished Me with a favourable Opportunity of Reducing the French Inhabitants . . . to a Proper Obedience to His Majesty and Governments, or forcing them to Quit the Country." It continued with a justification of the action on terms of military necessity and the concluding paragraphs said that since there were nearly seven thousand of them they could not just be given leave to depart. Such a course would have strengthened French power, so that

> it was Judged a Necessary, and the only Practicable Measure, to Divide them among the Colonies, Where they may be of Some Use as most of them Are Healthy Strong People; . . . And they May become Profitable and it is possible in time Faithful Subjects.[24]

With a final flourish, the letter expressed entire faith in the concurrence of its reader in the measures which had been taken, measures which resulted in the governor or lieutenant-governor of the colony in question reading the letter as the ships and their burdens waited his instructions in the harbour. The various colonial *Gazettes* had printed news of the passage of events in Nova Scotia from the time of the capture of Beauséjour in June, but no colony save Connecticut took much notice. The unreadiness of the rest was shown by the discussion caused in the respective legislative assemblies and among the councillors of the respective territories as the ships bearing the Acadians arrived. Each local government coped as best it could, the governors discussed the matter among themselves, the Gazettes commented and the Acadians suffered.

In describing the deportation some writers have suggested that families were deliberately split up. In assessing this charge it is necessary to bear in mind what the Acadian considered a family. They were used to being in close contact with several generations, great-grandparents to great-grandchildren, and to keeping in touch with the siblings. One of the Leblanc families, that headed by Daniel Leblanc, consisted of the grandparents, sixteen children and one hundred and two grandchildren. The old man, dying bewildered in Philadelphia, protesting to the end his loyalty to the English, wept because there were only sixteen of his descendants at his bedside.[25] If it is thought that there was a definite policy to separate husband and wife, parents and children, within the unit visualised in the twentieth-century as the nuclear family, then the charge is unfounded. There are a variety of recorded instances where English officers acted to prevent such an occurrence. But for the Acadians the nuclear family was almost unknown: they formed clans of multi-generational structure and these spread throughout their villages, no one village being the monoply of one family. Ships even from the same village were despatched to different destinations and, inevitably, brothers and sisters, grandparents and grandchildren, aunts and cousins, were separated. At the same time, although the Acadian families were disrupted in this fashion, the close-knit connections between the group as a whole meant that each separate shipload of Acadians would be interrelated. In other words, brothers and sisters might find themselves in widely separate towns, but at the same time find cousins and in-laws surrounding them.

The result of the deportation for the society as a whole was to break it into small groups which were disembarked at widely separated points on the North American continent. Ironically, Massachusetts, whose governor, Shirley, had supported the idea of the deportation, received one of the largest contingents of the exiles and kept them longest. But New York, Pennsylvania, Maryland, Virginia and the Carolinas, as well as Georgia, all had their quota of Acadians landed. In most cases, the reception given followed the pattern established by Massachusetts. In spite of the expense, and in spite of fears of the exiles' revolt, the people of the Commonwealth provided for their support and tried to settle them in various small towns and villages.

These efforts were mostly unsuccessful. The Acadians wandered about, looking for family and friends, in spite of all prohibitions to the contrary. More than one community, like that of Salem, complained that "by reason of this addition of Neutrals, the poor of our Town are kept out of the alm-house."[26] The type of support which the Acadians received is typified by the records of Medway, which spent £7.11s. 3d. to support nine people from October 28th, 1756 to March 7th, 1757. The full report reads as follows:

	£	s.	d.
To House Rent for One family from October 28th, 1756 to March 7th, 1757		2.	8.
To nine Bushels of rye meal	1.	10.	0.
To nine Bushels and one half of Indian meal and corn	1.	2.	9½.
To 286 pounds of Beef	1.	18.	1½.
To 64 pounds of Pork		8.	6½.
To 32 pounds of Cheese		5.	9½.
To 3 pounds of Butter		1.	10.
To 8 pounds of Mutton		1.	1.
To 10 gallons of Milk		4.	6.
To 13 loads of wood		13.	0.
To a bushel and a peck of Salt		1.	9.
To Bread			4.
To five gallons of Cyder		1.	2½.
To 2 pounds of Wool		4.	8.
To mending a pot			8.
To a wheel and an axe		16.	8.
To Mr. John Thibault for Trouble as an Interpretor			8.
	£7.	11.	3.

To this report was attached the explanatory note that the older people; in their late forties, were not well and were incapable of constant labour; that the eldest son and his wife, in their twenties, were well and healthy but that the younger members of the family were small and not capable of much. The men were all fishermen and could handle an axe but "do not understand our common husbandry: by reason thereof we can't find 'em Constant Labour."[27]

By the time of the Peace of Paris, 1763, Massachusetts computed that it had paid £9563. 9s. 10d. for the support of the Aca-

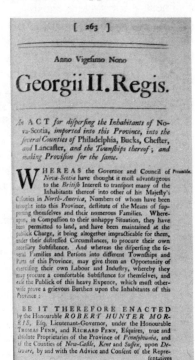

Note the printer of this law about the Acadian exiles.

dians exiled there. For all this money, the exiles remained alien to the community, and suffered an increasingly high death rate. This experience was the common denominator for almost all the other colonies. Administrations tried to settle the Acadians in small groups, and to provide for their children by following the custom of binding them out for apprentices. They were forced, in general, to accord the exiles much more freedom of movement than they wished and to support them in a similar manner to the provisions made for their own poor. Connecticut, New York, and Pennsylvania followed this pattern, although it is worth remarking that the Huguenot families of Philadelphia proved greater friends to the Catholic Acadians than might have been expected. Men like Benezet tried to enlist the services of the Penn brothers on their behalf.[28] The Acadians sent to Maryland ended, some years later, mostly in Louisiana, but they made that destination via Santo Domingo.[29] Those sent to Virginia were re-despatched immediately to England, the Virginians arguing that the Acadians were British subjects and entitled to support from London. In the Carolinas and Georgia the tale becomes even more confused, with the local administrations having much less than total control over the exiles.

The intentions of Lawrence and the English administrators of Nova Scotia had been to solve what they considered to be the strategic problem of their colony, and to render it a solid outpost of the English Crown. The consequence to the Acadians was an explosive disruption of their established community. By 1760 it looked as if the society they had built had been eradicated and as if it would only be a matter of time before those wandering in exile would succumb to their miseries or end assimilated by their new environments. For many Acadians this was precisely their fate.

Chapter V

Exile Rejected: 1755-1867

From the outset the Acadians saw their exile as undeserved. As the ships landed their burdens along the Atlantic shore, the exiles immediately set about stating their case to the colonial

. . . some returned to die. Baie St. Marie.

administrators. One man wrote to the Governor of Massachusetts that he and his family had "been employed in repairing the forts at Annapolis",[1] and that he himself had been

> an overseer of all Carts in bringing up Timber which I was obliged to do in the Night Time for fear of the Indians where I and my family run the risk of our Lives. . . . . Major Handfield . . . gave me my choice to remove where I pleased.

Similar letters can be found in the archives of all the Atlantic states, emphasizing that the writers had "always lived in a friendly manner with the English, and used to supply the garrison with food and a considerable quantity of provisions", or that they had always "entertained the most friendly sentiments" for the English. Handbills that summed up the Acadian point of view appeared at approximately the same time on the opposite sides of the Atlantic, in Philadelphia and in Rennes. There is little difference between the accounts given in the two widely separated towns. In the *Relation of the French Neutrals*, published in Philadelphia in 1758, the author writes:

> Almost numberless are the Instances which might be given of the Abuses and Losses we have undergone from the French Indians on Account of our strict Adherence to our Oath of Fidelity; and yet, notwithstanding our strict Observance thereof, we have not been able to prevent the grievous Calamity which is now upon us . . .[2]

In the *Relation de ce qui s'est passe an Acadie,* which was published in Rennes the previous year,* 1757, it is stated

> Les Acadiens sujets du Roi d'Angleterre par le cession du Roi de France, demanderent a rester neutres dans la Guerre qu'il y avoit entre les deux Puissances qu'ils aimoient et respectoient également.[3]

Later writings in France follow very much the same line, although those written by French authorities, as opposed to the memoirs of the Acadians themselves, are inclined to insist to a greater extent on the culpability of the English.

Perhaps the shortest summary of the Acadian position at this time, and one which can be taken as representative of them all, is the account of the Abbé Le Loutre, even though this was not written until 1768. The crucial event, the final meeting between

---

*Acadians came to France in different groups, some via one of the other English colonies, some via Quebec or St. Pierre and Miquelon. The greatest number were those via Virginia and England, who reached France in 1763-4, See *infra* this chapter.

English and Acadian, which led directly to the deportation, is described as follows:

> Le commandant Anglais leur dise qu'ils falloire prêter le serment de fidélité au Roy d'Angleterre, et prendre les armes pour la cause commune: la defence de la Patrie . . . les Acadiens demandent un moment de reflexion, on le leur accorder, ausitot [sic] ils jeteront tous à genoux et après une courte prière, un Viellard se levait et parlait au nom de tous. Nous avons déja prêté et signé le serment de fidélité et nous sommes tous prêt à le renouveler [sic], mais nous voulons conserver le privilège de Neutralité, qu'on nous a accordé, et nous ne prendrons jamais le serment contre La France.[4]

The account becomes more flowery as it goes on, but its main theme is clear: the Acadians were obedient to the English so long as they were permitted to remain neutral towards the French. In sum, the Acadians were convinced they had been the victims of an injustice.

This emotional sense of having been in the right, of having had unwarrantable sufferings inflicted upon them, was one source of strength for the Acadians in exile, and a partial explanation of the extraordinary capacity for survival which the majority of them showed. Despite the immediate inroads of death, the toll taken on board ship, the victims given to smallpox and yellow fever on shore, the high mortality rate among the new-born and the old during the first months of exile, the Acadians, as a group, showed incredible resilience. Before authorities in English North America as in England, before officials in Quebec as in France, they maintained the same stance: they were members of an entity that had a measure of independence from the wider policy attempting to administer their affairs. They were the "neutral French", "the Acadians", "de la Nation Acadienne", this last phrase being used by, among others, an old woman of eighty, who, at the time of her letter, had been resident in France for more than thirty years. But resistance to assimilation was based upon more than the emotional conviction of injustice, important though this was. It was due as much to characteristics which had been built into the Acadian society for more than a hundred years and it was strengthened by the way in which the Acadians were treated by the societies which newly surrounded them.

The family structure which had evolved during the seventeenth century, and which had absorbed into the group of original settlers each wave of newcomers after 1671, continued to flourish in exile. In the English colonies in North America, the barriers of language and religion supported the isolation of the Acadians, and most of the marriages recorded there are those between two Acadians. Some of these were second, or even third, marriages for one, if not both, partners, suggesting perhaps comfort sought in adversity. Among those Acadians whose fate led them to France, via England and Virginia, a journey taking several years, there were several marriages between Acadian women and "local" men, the latter including itinerant Irishmen and wandering Corsicans as well as English and Frenchmen. On the whole, the result of these marriages was an increase for the Acadians, the men following their wives. When a large number of those Acadians who had come to France gave up the attempt to establish themselves there and set out, under Spanish aegis, for Louisiana, such households continued to move with them. The documents recording this move contain much information about Acadian demography in exile, and the final records of the Acadians leaving Nantes destined for Louisiana, in 1785, show families of four generations, including great-grandparents in their eighties and year-old babies with teenage parents.[5]

The cohesion of the Acadians was further aided by the pattern of political life which they had experienced. Over and over again, documents refer to negotiations with the Acadians taking place with their "leading men", "les chefs de familles". Throughout their existence the Acadians had been used to a dual political structure: that of the village and that which linked the village to a wider administration. They had developed the use of particular individuals to speak in the name of the village, as for example in the case, in the late 1690s, of Beaubassin and the dissatisfaction with the priest appointed to that parish. With the English victory of 1710, this system became much more formalised with the use of deputies sent by the villages to Annapolis Royal and to Halifax. In exile, the Acadians benefited from being able to present a united front and to draw up petitions which gave the grievances and merits of their whole community. Eighteenth-century officials, meeting the Acadians for the first time, whether in North America or in Europe, were startled to discover Acadian willingness to argue, to discuss, and to propose alternatives to the official plans for their future. Although as individuals the Acadians found themselves divided from their nearest relatives, and part of an uprooted band of cousins and in-laws rather than siblings and parents, the Acadian society was broken into viable pieces, and not completely atomised.

The history of the Acadians in France shows this particularly clearly. The French government, at both the local and the central level, in the person of the King as well as in the persons of his Ministers, considered the Acadians as having bravely suffered for the love of France and as refugees particularly worthy of being established within the state. To this end, they were first granted a pension and then efforts were made to integrate them into the life of the nation. From the point of view of the officials in charge, it was a matter of establishing a new body of peasants, with the same fundamental conditions as the rest of the peasantry in the immediate neighbourhood. From the point of view of the Acadians, it was the rebuilding of their lives. They objected strongly to the remnants of feudalism which accompanied the grant of farms to them on Belle-Ile, the island off the coast of Brittany where the first attempt was made to establish the Acadians in France. They did not like the inspection of their lands to see if they were being farmed correctly, nor the rents taken in kind from crops and cattle. They objected to the request to build roads and to use communal mills and ovens. Above all, they could see no reason why they should not practise a certain a mount of capitalism. There is a long and complicated case, running through letters from the Abbé Le Loutre and the then governor of Belle-Ile, Warren, and involving the Parlement and Etats de Bretagne, which sprang from the wish of one Acadian to pay another to work his farm while he himself made a living in the nearest town. The French authorities considered the man a peasant, and one who must work the land for which he had contracted. The man in question, Babin, considered himself a man free to gain his bread however he wished. The final settlement of the case came with the man's departure to Louisiana. This example is one of the more exotic, but there is a general pattern of Acadian discontent with eighteenth-century France and although some settled, mainly as sailors, in Europe, many took advantage of the opportunity to recross the Atlantic when it came their way. Even such a man as Joseph Le Blanc, dit "Le Maigre", whose pro-French actitivies went back to the 1740s and who was granted a very high pension in France because of this, finally left and ended his life on Miquelon.[6]

And it is, of course, in North America, that the resilience of Acadian society showed itself most strongly. Nova Scotia was never entirely without Acadians, even during the last years of the 1750s. Once permission was given to resettle in Nova Scotia, they made their way back there with increasing swiftness. But on their arrival they were greeted with a bare tolerance from the authorities. The permission for them to resettle had been the result of exterior pressures upon Nova Scotia. It was fundamentally the result of a proposal put to the Acadians who were still in Nova Scotia by a French Protestant, Jacques Robin, in 1763. Governor Wilmot, who had arrived to take charge of Nova Scotia that same year, had informed the Lords of Trade that Robins had

> transmitted Letters to the leading persons among the Acadians inviting them in the strongest terms from all quarters, wherever dispersed to collect themselves at Miramicy to settle on these lands which, for their encouragement, he assures them of a very ample distribution and a sufficient supply of provisions.[7]

The immediate result in London was a representation drawn up by the Lords of Trade to the King, which reads in part

> . . . There is no doubt that the organisation of so large a body of useful Inhabitants would be of great advantage to and promote the speedy settlement of this valuable Province: and therefore we humbly submit to Your Majesty

whether it would not be more advisable to receive them into the Community under the Security of the Oath of Allegiance . . . than to aggravate their present resentments by absolutely prescribing [sic] them.. . .[8]

On July 16th, 1764, the Lords of Trade informed Wilmot that he should allow the Acadians to settle in Nova Scotia, provided they took the oath of allegiance, in spite of their "having taken up Arms in support of the Crown during the late War."[9]

Nor did this permission entail the resettlement of the Acadians upon their old lands. Although many of the Acadian farms had remained unoccupied for some years after 1755, new settlers had taken them over by 1760.* Further, they were still feared as a possible danger to the security of the province.

The committee in charge of the project suggested that they be given lands which "would prevent as much as possible them having any intercourse with ye Islands of St. Pierre and Miquelon."[10] Thus when one of the most important settlements was established by government order in 1767, it was in Clare County, on the Bay of Fundy shore and not the Atlantic coast. Its future inhabitants were collected together from all parts of the province, but particularly from the environs of Halifax. In 1768, the first of several groups of Acadians to return from Massachusetts joined the growing settlement. During the next decade the parish registers show a fairly steady stream of such wanderers coming to the parish, whose travels had included not only North America but also Europe. By 1771 the number of Acadian families reported within the

---

*There has been a continuous discussion as to who made money from the misery of the Acadians. It is highly likely that war profiteering entered into the picture at some point, but it has been conclusively proved (i) that Lawrence himself derived no financial benefit from the tragedy; (ii) that the lands in question were not immediately settled by New England troops, the latter being only too happy to return to their own villages, and that the actual settlement of them was a matter of quite considerable time. Brebner, *New England's Outpost* has a succinct account of this.

peninsula and along the north shore of the Bay of Fundy, as well as those on the Atlantic coast of New Brunswick, was 193 families, about two thousand people. Thirty years later the Acadians of Nova Scotia alone numbered eight thousand. From this point, the opening of the nineteenth century, the further increase of the Acadians in these regions was due to the preponderance of births over deaths, rather than to the return of further exiles.

Evidence as to the daily lives of the Acadians in Nova Scotia after 1764 can be found in the records of the archives of the Archbishop of Quebec. In 1768, the first missionary to be sent among them by Bishop Briand made a report. There was a considerable amount of drunkenness among them, especially those who had been at some time in Quebec. Those who had remained among the English were considered to be still very devout. But the great fault of the majority, the missionary wrote, was a considerable stubbornness, a refusal to be grouped together unless they were so inclined, and a refusal to take up land on any condition except a direct grant from the Crown. In North America, as in France, the Acadian would not accept a form of seigneurial control. In sum, as far as lay within their power, the Acadians who returned to the Maritimes after 1764 attempted to recreate the self-contained and independent life they had had before 1755.

In this they were to a large extent successful. They were aided in their design by the circumstances of their lives, the attitude of the authorities and the strength of their traditions. The geographical situation of their settlements, for the most part now the least attractive lands of the Maritimes, allowed an isolation which, if it meant material hardship, also meant cultural integrity. The Nova Scotia authorities made no attempt to assimilate them into the general life of the colony. There were no magistrates appointed among the Acadians, nor did their communities possess any form of municipal government dictated by an outside authority. Once more the Acadians were able to develop the political structure of their own villages in their own way. The neglect of the provincial authorities drew little or no protest from them. Despite their delight in litigation for its own sake, the Acadians were used to submitting their disputes to a higher authority only when they themselves wished so to do. Once more the spiritual charge of the Bishop of Quebec, their language and religion, education and moral attitudes were the provenance of a source other than that which supplied the majority of their neighbours. The division between Acadians and other Maritimers was nurtured as much by themselves as by external factors.

At one point, in 1795, the Scottish immigrants of Prince Edward Island wrote to the Acadians,

> Before we had departed our native country we had heard of your destitute Case and moreover that all of you in the Island would settle with any who should bring you a clergyman: We believe the two objects of relieving you and your settling with us, concurred in determining out leaders to prefer this Island to any other part of America. Had you accordingly thought proper to Assimilate with us after our arrival, we might probably e'en now have been enabled to fall upon a plan of being more adequately provided with clergy . . . but you kept all along as before in a dispersed state mostly in the remote parts of the Island.[11]

Another commentator, an old settler who had lived in Nova Scotia before, during, and after the deportation, remarked in 1791:

> . . . we find them still steadfast in their religious Tenets, maintaining almost an inviolate Separation from all other classes of People and in every respect answering (very nearly) the same character as the first.[12]

By the opening of the nineteenth century, then, the Acadians of Nova Scotia, New Brunswick and Prince Edward Island had settled down into their own communities. Deportation and exile had not eradicated the society built during the seventeenth and early eighteenth century. The individuals whose ancestors had been the first settlers of this "continental cornice" had retained as a heritage not merely gifts from an individual nuclear family but also traditional links which bound them into a much larger group. Whatever the nineteenth century would bring to the Acadians, it would be faced by many of them from the standpoint of members of a community. The political strategy which had been developed by them in the past, methods of dealing with superior forces by negotiation through the unity of the village, would be used in the future. As the years went by, the cohesion of the Acadians was noted and recognised. In 1828, an emigration guide to the Maritimes specifically stated that the "Acadian French would always settle in groups".[13] The dominant English-Protestant society, which surrounded the Acadians, found their assimilation a most complex matter. To the development of the relations between the different groups of settlers, to the divisions of language and religion, geography and economy, which have already been described, the Acadians added another barrier which opposed their integration, and one of even greater power: their own concept of the deportation.

As early as 1771 it was noticed that it was customary in the Acadian villages for memories and experiences of the deportation to be recounted in the evenings. The practice, in itself not surprising, produced a greater unity of attitude than might have been expected. It produced a considerable measure of agreement among the Acadians as to what exactly had happened in 1755. For some time the tradition remained unwritten. Its consolidation into a widely accepted literary form was the work of the poet from Maine, Longfellow. He first heard the story in 1840 or 1841 and he took six or seven years to write a poem about it, which he called "Evangeline". He noted that the authorities he used "in writing Evangeline were the Abbé Raynal and Mr. Haliburton: the first for the pastoral simple life of the Acadians; the second for the history of their banishment." Raynal was a member of the French Encyclopaedists of the eighteenth century. Into the ten-volume *Histoire Philosophique et Politique de l'Etablissement et du commerce des Européens dans les deux Indés,* published in Paris in 1766, he introduced an account of the deportation of the Acadians in Volume VI.

Owing a great deal to eighteenth-century delight in the sense of classical organisation and pastoral civilisation, Raynal provided Longfellow with a picture worthy of Virgil's *Georgics*, "Ah, blest beyond all bliss the husbandmen, did they but know their happiness. On whom, far from the clash of arms, the most just Earth showers from her bosom a toil-less substance." Haliburton, when he wrote his *Historical and Statistical Account of Nova Scotia*, was both a member of the Nova Scotia legislature and a struggling young lawyer. His major concern was to produce something that would erase the "ill favoured brat" image of the province. However, the fourth chapter of his work, which covered the years 1748 to 1755, was Longfellow's source for the quantity of details concerning the deportation of the Acadians which he includes in "Evangeline". The crystallization into poetry, by an American from Maine, of a legend passed on in a dinner conversation by the Reverend Connelly, with the addition of materials supplied by an eighteenth-century priest of liberal tendencies and a nineteenth-century Nova Scotian lawyer gave the Acadians their most vivid artistic symbol of their past.

The way in which the Acadians adopted Longfellow's poem as the incarnation of their idea of their past is connected with the development of their educational structure. Before the mid-nineteenth century the Acadians were predominantly illiterate, one visitor from France reporting that they were without newspapers and almost without schools. It was not until 1854 that the first co-educational parochial school was established at St. Thomas, Memramcook. Its founder, Father La France, appealed for help for his efforts because, as he wrote to a friend, "Vous savez que le pauvre peuple Acadien n'a jamais eu justice jusqu'à présent du côte de l'éducation."[14] His work ended literally in flames, but from the ashes rose the College of St. Joseph, founded 10th October, 1864. The graduates of such institutions became the professional men of the Acadians.

From the beginning St. Joseph's was more than merely a diocesan seminary. Of the nine students who began their third year of studies in the fall of 1866, five became priests, one a lawyer, one a doctor, one a teacher and the last a storekeeper. The lawyer was Pascal Poirier, who entered the federal Senate in 1885, and although appointed for New Brunswick was always known as the Senator of the Acadians. Further investigation of later graduates shows that the majority returned to their villages. With them they took back not only professional qualifications, but also ideas about what it meant to be an Acadian. Throughout the college Longfellow's "Evangeline" was taught. It was used as a text in Rhetoric by the students in 1865. Pascal Poirier later said that for more than two years he carried a copy of the poem on him, close to his heart, and that during long walks "j'en recetais à haute voix des chants entiers."[15] The first Acadian newspaper, *Le Moniteur Acadien,* began life as a weekly, published out of Shediac, New Brunswick and with its first issues was distributed a copy of the French-Canadian translation of "Evangeline". This was in 1867, and motto across the front page was "Notre langue, notre religion et nos coutumes."

From the late 1860s on, the connections between the Acadians and "Evangeline" become commonplace. The personages of the poem attained the stature of historical beings. But the creation of the poet was less those vibrant characters than the presentation of a society's dream. The strength of the poem is land, countryside and a way of life, and its popularity among the Acadians was the precise extent to which they were convinced that the poet's idea of their national character, and of the events of the deportation, matched their own concepts of both. The dominating theme of Longfellow's vision is that of terrestrial Paradise Lost, and one lost without proven original sin. He includes only such political material as adds to a picture of "patient Acadian farmers." The notary, one of the chief characters, father of Evangeline, is represented as once having endured "suffering much in an old French fort as the friend of the English." The only explanation of the action of the English is a short speech made by an officer to the assembled Acadians:

"You are convened this day", he said, "by his majesty's orders. Clement and kind has he been; but how you have

answered his kindness Let your own hearts reply!
To my natural make and my temper Painful the task
is I do, which to you I know must be grievous Yet must I
bow and obey, and deliver the will of our monarch;
Namely, that all your lands, and dwellings and cattle of
all kinds Forfeited be to the Crown; and that you your-
selves from this province be transported to other lands.
God grant you may dwell there ever as faithful subjects,
a happy and peaceable people!
Prisoners, now I declare you; for such is His Majesty's
pleasure."[16]

The extent to which "Evangeline" became the unchallenged
repository of historical truth in the eyes of the Acadians is further revealed by the speeches given by them at their own conventions. At the first of these in Memramcook, Wednesday,
July 20th, 1880, the poem was quoted as historical fact, and the
idea that the Acadians had been unjustly expelled by people
to whom they had every intention of being loyal was continuously underlined. The 1880s saw two more Acadian confer-
ences and this theme was repeated: "L'Acadie n'a d'autre
histoire national que la siene propre et celle de la France."[17] As
a result of these conventions the Acadians emerged with a national saint, a national flag and a national feast day, all different
from those chosen as symbols by Quebec during the same period
of years. There is no doubt that the Acadians considered themselves a unique people, not to be confused with other groups of
basically French descent; a people who, as one of their leading
men averred at the time of Confederation, knew nothing of
"Bas Canada, sinon qu'il avait, à Québec et à Montréal, des
Français qui s'appellaient des Canadiens."[18] Against considerable odds, a small community had survived a major disruption
and a consequent political dominance by people of another
language and religion. Their story ends where it began. How
was this achievement gained without a much more radical
political programme?

Acadian "Nationalism"

In the summer months of 1968 the Acadians of Cheticamp, a village on the north coast of Cape Breton Island, set out to persuade the education minister of Nova Scotia to provide their schools with Grade X textbooks in French. Textbooks in French

Men do not live by bread alone . . . .

for subjects other than that language were in use in the lower grades, but the community wished to see their children taught in the same manner in the last years of high school. As part of the campaign the village was decorated with Acadian flags and the arguments presented to the minister made considerable references to the past history of the Acadians. Arguments drawn from Quebec, from France, or from Canadian federal support for bilingualism were in the minority. The people of Cheticamp were asking for the use of French in the schools because it was their language because they were Acadians. French-speaking, Catholic, descendants of the first European settlers of the lands which today are divided between Nova Scotia, New Brunswick, Prince Edward Island and the northeastern section of the American state of Maine, the Acadians at the end of the 1960s still preserve a way of life in the Maritime provinces which is in many aspects different from that led by their English-speaking neighbours, whether Protestant or Catholic. The struggle of the people of Cheticamp resembled many other such struggles undertaken by the Acadians in the Maritime provinces, both before and after Confederation. A striking similarity of attitude unites all such efforts: while claiming cultural objectives, the Acadians rarely, if ever, used arguments which would entail the separation of the Acadians from the control of their present government. Their belief in their community, their desire to preserve their traditions, their language and their religion, all objectives stated in so many words by the founder of one of the first Acadian newspapers at the time of Confederation, were not attached to pressure for an *"Acadie libre"*.

Part of the explanation of the Acadian attitude lies in their realization of their political and economic position within the Maritimes after 1755. Whatever else that year meant, or came to mean, in Acadian history, it meant their conquest. The vast majority of the Acadian community then in existence were forcibly ejected from their lands and sent into exile. Although this exile was for many only temporary, its consequence, even for those who returned to Nova Scotia and the lands which would be named New Brunswick and Prince Edward Island, was an enduring political weakness for the Acadian. Before the advent of universal suffrage, oligarchical governments, English-speaking and Protestant, paid little attention to the Acadians, except to ensure that as a group they would not raise a revolt.

After the advent of universal suffrage, demography made the Acadians, until recently, a minority group within each of the Maritime provinces. The economic consequences of the deportation were akin to its political aftermath: the Acadians found themselves able to make a living from the new lands allotted to them but for the majority it was a living of a much lower stan-

War Memorial, 1914-18, Cheti-camp. There was no conscription crisis here.

dard than the one they had known before 1755. This description of the Acadian appreciation of their circumstances, however, raises a great number of questions about the Acadians as a people, for it suggests the existence of a self-conscious society, with cultural and social distinctiveness rejecting the ambition of founding a nation state, a rare, if not unique, control of emotion by reason. The twentieth-century belief in the principle of "national self-determination" as the foundation of the constitutions of states forces one to ask for the emotional reasons why the Acadians do not demand an *"Acadie libre"* if they have a basic sense of identification as Acadians.

The answer lies in the way in which the Acadians have not only developed their vision of themselves through the concept of their history, but also used this vision to face contemporary political challenges. The exigencies of any particular decade throughout their history found the Acadians prepared to argue the immediate issue with an appeal to precedent. Although the colony which they built changed hands fourteen times during the seventeenth century, before being finally absorbed into the British empire, the Acadians managed to develop their own society and in so doing to cope with the demands of alien, transitory administrators, whether these were sent to them by the French or the English. From a very early stage in their development, the Acadians acted with a sense of the independent existence of their community, a belief that the life of their villages was more than just an offshoot of the life of the particular European power whose constitutional charge they at the moment happened to be. Between 1604 and 1715 these former Europeans, the settlers of the colony called "Acadie or Nova Scotia" in the international treaties of the time, founded their villages and organized their daily concerns with a considerable measure of self-government. In matters where they had to submit in some measure to an outside authority, the Acadians showed a great ability to negotiate by means of delegates sent in their name to the momentarily stronger power. The immediate political question, whether about the manner of registering titles to new land, or the question of prayers after mass for Louis XIV or the form of an oath of allegiance to be sworn to either France or England, was always discussed by the Acadians with reference to past actions. Despite the fact that the settlers were not all from one part of France, nor even all from France itself, as they farmed the land the Acadians created their own community.

And of course they remain a community today. Any conversation with the administrative officers of the Société Nationale Acadienne, whose head-quarters are in Moncton, New Brunswick, makes this perfectly clear. The French-speaking Catholics of the Maritime provinces who trace their ancestry to those who were involved in the deportation of 1755 are united by a strong love of their land, by a wish to feel rightfully its people. If, during 1972, they argue with Mayor Jones about the need for a bilingual plaque at city hall, it is because they wish to feel that Moncton is as much part of their environment as Buctouche, as Cap Pélé. The Acadian of the nineteen-seventies is like the Acadian of the sixteen-seventies: for both, the place where they live is the place they like to live. For both, the question is how can they maintain their particular ways on this particular land.

The sturdiness of Acadian culture has perhaps been overlooked because, until recently, it has been largely analphabetic. Yet the traditions of Acadian living are as vigorous as those of any small people: hospitable, gay, with a poetic appreciation of landscape and sea-scape, the Acadians welcome any who come to them with a desire to know what the Acadians themselves feel. They are less considerate of those who came merely to analyze the Acadian situation, to point out what Acadian politics should be, and to criticize when the Acadians refuse to accept wholesale tactics sketched closer to the St. Lawrence than to the Bay of Fundy. Canadian life is immeasurably richer because of the existance of Acadian uniqueness.

Bibliographical Note

The most recent bibliography for Acadian studies is that by M-A Tremblay in *Situation de la recherche sur le Canada français,* (Quebec) 1964. It should be supplemented by the references in the section of the *Canadian Historical Review* entitled "Recent Publications relating to Canada". Mason Wade, whose monumental work on the French Canadians has proved a valuable source book for scholars of that subject, is to publish an almost equally lengthy work on Maritime history within the current year. This will certainly provide very valuable reference material for anyone working in Acadian history.

In the meantime the best short introduction to Acadian history still remains A. Doughty's *The Acadian Exiles* (Toronto) 1916. It is attractively written and gives a good overview of the general problems of Acadian history. For the story written from the viewpoint of power politics, J. B. Brebner's *New England's Outpost: Acadia before the Conquest of Canada* (New York), 1927 is outstanding. A geographer's attitude to the way in which the colony developed is presented by A. H. Clark in *Acadia: The Geography of Early Nova Scotia to 1760* (Madison, Milwaukee and London) 1968. This is an excellent account of many of the economic factors of Acadian history for the period under review, but suffers occasionally from historical inaccuracy. The concluding discussion of the extent to which the Acadians demonstrate the Turner thesis of the frontier in American history is interesting, if controversial. As has been suggested throughout this text, the deportation itself has been the subject of some two hundred books. In *The Acadian Deportation: De-*

86

liberate Perfidy or Cruel Necessity? (Toronto) 1969, I made an attempt to bring together the main examples of differing historical judgements on the matter and to present as well as many of the most crucial primary documents relating to 1755 as space would allow.

If this bibliographical note is short it is not the lack of published works which governs but the lack of works still in print. Many of the studies written about the Acadians at the end of the nineteenth century and the beginning of the twentieth century are now unavailable. Perhaps the one to obtain at all costs would be the copy of the 1905 *Report of the Public Archives of Canada,* in which the then Dominion Archivist, Placide Gaudet, printed a rich collection of materials about the Acadians, gathered from archives in Europe as well as in North America. If readers can obtain either the works of Rameau de St. Père, who published in the middle of the ninteenth century, or Emile Lauvrière, who published in 1922, they will be both fortunate and entertained. Their style of history is very like that of Francis Parkman, the great nineteenth-century American historian, whose works *A Half Century of Conflict* and *Montcalm and Wolfe* are concerned in part with the history of the Acadians. All these historians are concerned with the political aspects of the question and write with the verve of committed beliefs.

Finally, the wide field of periodical literature should be explored. Once again the references in the *Canadian Historical Review* prove to be the best starting point for the student.

Notes

Permission for excerpts quoted has been obtained. The following are the abbreviations used in these notes.

A.A.Q. Archives de l'Archevêque de Québec
B.M. British Museum
B.N. Bibliothèque Nationale
N.S.A. Nova Scotia Archives; if the reference is prefaced by
P.A.C., Public Archives of Canada; collection is available in Ottawa; if otherwise, collection is in Halifax.

Report: this refers to the official reports published by the Public Archives of Canada, the date which follows giving the year in question.

Introduction

1. Speech given at the first Acadian convention in 1881, printed in Robidoux ed. *Convention Nationales Des Acadiens* (Shediac) 1907, translation N.E.S.G.

Chapter I

1. Brebner, J. B.: *New England's Outpost*, (1927), p. 16.
2. The origin of the name has been the matter of endless debate. The best that can be said about it has been summarized by E. H. Wilkins in an article in *Proceedings of the American Philosophical Society*, Vol. 101, No. 1 (1957), pp. 4-30, entitled "Arcadie in America" from which the following is an extract:
" . . . on several maps that are certainly or probably of the third quarter of the sixteenth century the name *Larcadie* or *Arcadie* appears as regional name below

or to the right of a regional name meaning New France: that on a map published in 1586 the name *Arcadie* is applied specifically to Nova Scotia . . . that a map made by Levasseur in 1601 bears the name *Coste de Cadie* in association with but to the left of, the name *Nouvelle France...* that . . . the whole region (at the opening of the seventeenth century) is variously named as *lacadie, Lacadie, La Cadie, Lacadye, acadie* and *la cadye; . . .* Reprinted by permission of the American Philosophical Society.
3. Patent, Nov. 1603; P.A.C., C 11 A, I, p. 78; Commission, Jan. 29, 1605, P.A.C. C 11 A, p. 58.
4. Qt. Bishop, M: *Champlain The Life of Fortitude*, Carleton Library Edition, (1963), p. 82.
5. Lescarbot, A.: *Nova Francia*, (London), 1928, p. 93. Reprinted by permission of Routledge & Kegan Paul Ltd.
6. Bernard, A.: *Le Drame Acadien Depuis 1604*, (1936), p. 27.
7. Lescarbot, M.: *Histoire de la Nouvelle France suivie des Muses de la Nouvelle-France*, (Paris), 1866, vol. III. p. 30.
8. *Report*, P.A.C., 1886, Note B, p. cliv.
9. *Royal letters, Charters and Tracts relating to the colonisation of New England, etc., 1621-1638*, (Edinburgh) 1867, p. 120-123.
10. Archives Ille et Vilaine, La Rochelle: B. 5598. This collection of documents has been copied for the Public Archives of Canada.
11. Although the mathematics are incorrect, there is no supposition

of forgery. It is part of the Cardinal's papers in the B.N., Nouv. Acq. fr.: 5131, p. 102.
12. B.N.: Nouv. Acq. Fr.: 9282.
13. B.N.: Ancien fonds fr.: f. 18593. f. 390-393.
14. One of the best discussions of this in print is in Massignon, G.: *Les Parlers Francais d'Acadie* (Paris), 1965, Vol. I. p. 37.
15. Goubert, P.: *Cent mille Provinciaux au xvii siècle* (1968) p. 62.
16. These censuses have been frequently published. One of the best sources to consult, because of the interesting deductions presented with the material, is the work of Rameau de St. Père. In *La France aux colonies* (1859) the 1671 census is printed and in *Une colonie feodale en Ameririque-l'Acadie* (1889) the others are given.
17. P.A.C.: C 11 D: Relation d'Acadie . . . 29 Aug. 1686.
18. Parkman, F.: *A Half-Century of Conflict* Collier Ed. 1962, p. 363.
19. Lauvrière, E.: *La Tragédie d'un Peuple* (Paris) 1922, t. I, p. 185.
20. Shortt, Johnston and Lanctot, *Documents relating to Currency, Exchange and Finance in Nova Scotia . . . 1675-1758* (1933), p. 16.

Chapter II

1. Brebner, J. B.: *New England's Outpost*, (New York), 1927, p. 16-17.
2. *ibid.*
3. The most recent publication of the Treaty of Utrecht is in Israel, F.L. ed: *Major Peace Treaties of Modern History, 1748-1967*, (New York), 1967, Vol. I, p. 177.
4. This is in P.A.C.: MG11, N.S.A:4. There is a published version in Doughty, A.: *The Acadian Exiles*, (Toronto), 1916, p. 28-29.
5. P.A.C.: C. 11 D, . . . Relation: 9th August, 1686.
6. P.A.C.; C. 11 D., July, 1686.
7. P.A.C.: N.S.A.: 6.
8. Bernard, A.: *Le Drame Acadien* (Montreal), 1936, p. 254.

9. Akins, T. B., ed. *Selections from the Public Documents of the Province of Nova Scotia . . .* (Halifax), 1869, p. 158-160.
10. Brebner, J. B.: *op. cit.* p. 97.
11. Akins, *op. cit.* p. 139.
12. *Collections de Documents Inédits sur le Canada et l'Amerique,* 1889, vol. II, p. 80.
13. *ibid.*
14. *ibid.*
15. P.A.C.: N.S.A. 27.
16. Archibald, A.: "Expulsion of the French Acadians from Nova Scotia", in *Collections of the Nova Scotia Historical Society,* Vol. V, p. 59.
17. B. M. Brown Mss. 19071: Oct. 14th, 1742.
18. A.A.Q.: Lettres II, 523: Pontbriand au Ministre, 9 nov. 1746.
19. The population of the Acadians is a matter of considerable debate; this figure is an approximation from a consideration of both the French and English documentation on the subject.
20. A.N.: F. 23; Commerce.
21. Akins, *op. cit.* p. 139.
22. P.A.C.: Corres. Ile Royale: Chambon au Ministre, 25 Nov. 1744.
23. A.A.Q.: G. III/106: La Galissonière, 19th mai, 1752.
24. N.S./109: Council meeting records, containing the declaration of the new Governor, Cornwallis, 14th July, 1749.

Chapter III

1. Qtd. in Gipson, L. H.: *The British Empire before the American Revolution,* (New York) 1942, Vol. V, p. 304.
2. *Report,* P.A.C. 1905, II, App. C. p. 49-52.
3. N.S. 106: Council records; partially printed Akins, *op. cit.* p. 116.
4. N.S. 106: Council meeting records.
5. A.N.: C 11 A 93; partially printed in Lauvrière, E.; *La Tragédie d'un peuple,* Paris, 1922 Vol. I, p. 375.

89

6. N.S. 209: partially printed in translation, Akins, *op. cit.* p. 175-6.
7. N.S.A.: 34, printed in Akins. *op. cit.* p. 561-64.
8. Qtd. Gipson, L. H., *op. cit.* p. 194.
9. *ibid.* p. 192.
10. This ordnance has been published in full with an introduction by Brebner, J. B., in the *Canadian Historical Review* under the title "Canadian Policy towards the Acadians", Vol. XII, 1931.
11. A.A.Q.: Lettres II, Pontbriand, Nov. 9th, 1746.
12. A.A.Q.: Vicaire Générales, III, 133: Paris, 24th June, 1752.
13. P.A.C. N.S.A.: 49, Oct. 16th, 1752.
14. P.A.C.: N.S.A.: 49, Oct 1st, 1753.
15. P.A.C.: N.S.A.: 55, Aug. 1st, 1754.

Chapter IV

1. Gipson, L. H. *The British Empire before the American Revolution,* (New York), 1942, Vol. VI, p. 265.
2. P.A.C.: N.S.E., No. 7; E i No. 6.
3. P.A.C.: N.S.B. 8: These are the references to the Council meetings which are held by the archives in Ottawa. The Halifax archives reference would be N.S.: 187. These records have been printed in full in Griffiths, N.E.S.: *The Acadian Deportation: Deliberate Perfidy or Cruel Necessity?* (Toronto) 1969, p. 118-124.
4. P.A.C.: N.S.A.: 58.
5. *Report,* P.A.C., 1905, II, App. C. p. 61-2.
6. P.A.C., Northcliffe Collection, Vol. VIII, printed *in toto* in *Report,* P.A.C. 1926, p. 80-83.
7. Lauvrière, E.: *La Tragédie d'un Peuple,* (Paris), 1922, t. I, p. 83.
8. Brebner, J. B.: *New England's Outpost,* (New York) 1927, p. 225-6.
9. Columbia, South Carolina Council Journals, p. 480.
10. Library of Congress, Washington, Vernon-Wager Mss.
11. *ibid.*

12. B. M. Brown Mss., f. 19071, No. 55.
13. Boston, Municipal Library: September 23, 1755.
14. This journal has been fully published in the *Collections* of the Nova Scotia Historical Society, III, 1883, p. 71 *et seq.* Excerpts from it and some letters from Winslow are also in *Reports,* P.A.C. II, 1905, App. B.
15. P.A.C. II, 1905, App. B, p. 21.
16. *Reports,* P.A.C. II, App. B, p. 25.
17. Published in pamphlet form, 1889, Quebec.
18. *Reports,* P.A.C. II, App. B, p. 30.
19. Doughty, A.: *The Acadian Exiles* (Toronto), 1916, p. 153.
20. Council Minutes, Halifax, N.S. 187.
21. P.A.C.: N.S.A.: 55; April 14th, 1756.
22. P.A.C.: C.O. 5: vol. 211; copy in B.M. Add. Mss. Vol. 19073, f. 42.
23. P.A.C.: C.O. 218/5, B 1115.
24. *Reports,* P.A.C. II, 1905, App. B, p. 15-16.
25. Petition to the King of Great Britain, c. 1760, printed Smith, *Acadia: A Lost Chapter In American History* (Boston), 1884.
26. Boston State House, Hutchinson Papers. Vol. 23, Jan. 15th, 1757.
27. *ibid.*
28. Pennsylvania Historical Society: Pemberton Papers Vol. I, Aug. 20, 1760.
29. Bordeaux, Dept. de la Gironde, 4328/3rd avril, 1765.

Chapter V

1. *Report,* P.A.C., 1905, Vol. II. App. E, p. 100.
2. Hazard, ed., *Pennsylvania Archives,* First Series, Vol. III, 1852, p. 655.
3. This is a scruffy four-page pamphlet, anonymous, no date, annotated by the archivist at Ille et Vilaine, France, who places its publication in 1757.
4. Bordeaux, Mss. 1480, f. 28.
5. Archives Loire Inferieure, Nantes, Shipping Registers, 1785.

6. This information comes from the archives of Morbihan, Vannes, the most useful series being Serie 52153 and the Warren papers.
7. N.S.A.: 72; Dec. 10th, 1763.
8. P.A.C.: Biii5 from C.O. 218/6, June 19th, 1764.
9. *ibid.* July 16th, 1764.
10. B. N. Brown Mss. Add. Mss. f. 19071, 28th Sept., 1764.
11. A.A.Q.: I.P.E. 114: February 18th, 1795.
12. B. N. Brown Mss. Add. Mss. 19071, No. 58.
13. Macgregor J.: *Historical and Descriptive Sketches of the Maritime Colonies of British North America* (London) p. 125.
14. *Album Souvenir des Noces d'argent de la Société St. Jean-Baptiste du College St. Joseph.* (Memramcook) p. 97.
15. Qtd. Martin, E.: *L'Evangeline et la suite merveilleuse d'un poeme* (Paris) 1936, p. 222.
16. This reference is to the Walsh edition of the poem (Cambridge) 1909, p. 109-110.
17. Robidoux, ed. *Conventions Nationales des Acadiens* (Shediac), 1907, p. xi.
18. *ibid.*

Dates

Arrival of de Monts expedition at Ste. Croix, 1604.

Establishment of Port Royal, 1605.

Samuel Argall's raid, 1613.

Acadie receives additional title of Nova Scotia, 1621.

English and Scots dominate the colony, 1628-1632.

Razilly begins work for France in Acadie, 1632.

English rule the colony, 1654-1670.

Colony held again by France, 1670-1710.

Port Royal captured by Nicholson, rechristened Annapolis Royal, 1710.

Treaty of Utrecht awards the colony to the British, 1713.

Arrival of Cornwallis as governor with instructions to found Halifax, 1748.

Charles Lawrence appointed lieutenant-governor, 1753.

Deportation of the Acadians, 1755.

Acadians granted the right to own land once more in Nova Scotia, 1764.

First Acadian convention at Memramcook, 1881.

Index

Acadian: attitude to British occupation after Treaty of Utrecht, 21; characteristics of, 21-22; cohesion of people, 32, 33, 34; consciousness of political fluctuations, 48; contrasting interpretations by historians on way of life, 16; decision not to emigrate after Utrecht, 25; discontent with eighteenth-century France, 72-73; founding of St. Joseph, 78; geographical, 2; origins of people, 2, 3; reaction to deportation, 59; relations to Indians, 5; religious concerns, 46; resettlement in Nova Scotia and New Brunswick, 73, 74, 75, 76; strategy of neutrality, 23; years of neutrality, 39

Acadie: discussion of boundaries, 19; first census of, 15; growth of mixed economy in, 9; relations with New England, 17; tradition of lack of support for, 9

Aix-la-Chapelle: significance for Acadians, 39.

Alexander, Sir William: granted colonization rights by England, 10.

Argall, Samuel: sacking St. Saveur and Port Royal, 9

d'Aulnay de Charnisay, Charles de Menou: battles with la Tour, 12; death, 12; second in command to Razilly, 12

Beausejour: Acadians persuaded to go there, 44; capture by Moncton, 52; new French fort built, 43

Bernard, Antoine: Acadians do not wish to leave land in 1713, 25

Biencourt, Charles de: fur-trading; 1610, 7

Boscawen: arrival in Halifax, 54; present at Council meeting with Acadians, 56; retention of volunteer troops, 54

Brebner, J. B: on Acadians as neutral, 27; on interpretation of Lawrence, 58; on limits of colony, 19; views on Acadie, 16

Champlain, Samuel de: description of first winter in Acadia, 4

Cornwallis, Edward: arrival as governor, 40; instructions, 42; letter describing impact of French on the Acadians, 43

Deportation: confinement of Acadian delegates, 53; decision to deport reaffirmed, 55; document produced for legality of deportation, 56; Lawrence's letter on method to be used, 56-57; numbers deported, 60; reaction of British officials, 58, 59; separation of families examined, 64-65

Duerchville, Marquise de: right to colonise all Acadie granted, 8

Haliburton: account of deportation, 78

Hebert, Louis: daughter first Acadian, 6

Hopson, Peregrine: governor of Nova Scotia in 1753, 48; relation with French of Louisbourg, 48

Isle Royale: Acadian decision not to emigrate, 25; reluctance of British to let Acadians depart for, 25

Jesuits: arrival in Acadie, 8; clash with Poutrincourt, 8; counsel to Marie de Medici, 8; mission at St. John River mouth, 10

Kirke brothers: arrival of and capture of de la Tour, 11

La Rochelle: sea-port, importance to Acadie, 7

Lauvriere, Emile: interpretation of Lawrence, 57; views on British treatment of the Acadians; views on the Acadians, 16

Lawrence, Charles: administrator of Nova Scotia, 49; background and beliefs, 49, 50, 53; failure to capture Beauséjour, 46; final confrontation, 56; letter to governors of British colonies in North America, 63; prevents entry of French into Nova Scotia, 45

Le Loutre: assessment of Acadian position, 69-70; backed by abbé de l'Isle Dieu, 47; background, 43; burning of Beaubassin, 44; influence on the Acadians, 45

Lescarbot, Marc: assessment of needs of Acadie, 7.

Longfellow: Acadian belief in tradition of Evangeline, 79; writing of Evangeline, 77

Louisbourg: Acadian connection with, 45; capture of, 39

Mascerene, Paul: historians comment on, 31; letter on Acadian spirit, 32; letter to Governor Shirley, 30; letter to Philipps re Acadian attitude during hostilities in 1744, 30; meeting with Cornwallis, 40; statement of provisions of neutrality taken for granted by Acadians, 24; testimony to Acadian neutrality, 41

Micmacs: burning of Beaubassin, 44; composition of tribes, 4, 5; seen as menace by Cornwallis, 43

Monts, Sieur de, Pierre du Gost: charter given to, 3; revoked, 6

Oath: Acadian answer about, 43; Acadian offer to take unqualified, 57; Acadians refuse, 27; Acadians submit own version of, 29; Acadian traditional position stated, 54, 55; acceptable as long as neutrality granted, 23; Cornwallis' view on, 40, 41; English dilatoriness about, 49; grounds for Acadian belief, 27; Lawrence work for unqualified, 49; settled to Acadian satisfaction, 27

Parkman, Francis: views on Acadians, 16-17

Perrot: observation on Acadians 1686, 15, 16

Philipps, Governor: Acadian appeal to his memory, 55; thinks idea of oath with provisions better than nothing, 27

Port Royal (Annapolis Royal): British control after 1710, 20, 21; capture by English 1654, 14; de Monts charter revoked, 6; founding of settlement, 4; sacked by Virginian pirate, 8

Poutrincourt, Sieur de: determination to make Port Royal succeed, 6; relationship with French authorities, 7

Queen Anne: letter to administrators of colony 1713, 20.

Raynal, abbé: earliest account of deportation printed, 77

Razilly, Isaac de: cousin of Richelieu, 12; repatriates Scots settlers, 12

Richelieu, Cardinal: letter from Charles de la Tour, 11

Ste Croix Island: description of first winter on, 4

Shirley, Governor: correspondence with Lawrence, 51; interest in Aix-la-Chapelle negotiations, 39; letter from Mascerene re Acadian fidelity, 30

de la Tour, Charles: battles with d'Aulnay, 12; controversy over motives, 11; fur trade rights given to by Biencourt, 8; marries d'Aulnay's widow, 12; titles from Europe, 11

Utrecht, treaty of: question of boundaries, 19; terms for Acadians, 20

Vetch, Samuel: practice established of Acadian delegates, 25; question of value of Acadians, 26